99 Things to Do Betwee

Peter Graystone works for the Church Army. His job is to encourage churches to be visionary and imaginative about how to take the Good News beyond the wall of their churches and create Christian communities among people who need a fresh expression of the Gospel. This follows years working for Christian Aid, Scripture Union, and Emmanuel Church, Croydon. He still lives close to the church, surrounded by his godchildren, in a flat in which the teenagers of the congregation seem to be permanently camped out. To escape from it he turns off his mobile phone and goes to the theatre far too often!

Also by Peter Graystone and available from Canterbury Press:

Detox Your Spiritual Life in 40 Days

'Perhaps the greatest accolade that I can give this book is simply this: it works . . . This is connected spirituality, not pie-in-the-sky fantasy.' *UKCBD Reviews*

'. . . an easy-to-dip-into book with lots of humour alongside wise counsel and practical exercises to help us enjoy being a Christian every day of the week.' *Woman Alive*

'. . . an imaginative way into prayer and the spiritual disciplines.' *Christian Marketplace*

'. . . humorous, thoughtful, entertaining and interesting.' *Lion & Lamb*

Signs of the Times: The Secret Lives of Twelve Everyday Icons

'A well-written, smart, quick-paced book.' *Christian Marketplace*

'Fascinating and extremely accessible.' *Third Way*

www.canterburypress.co.uk

99 Things to Do Between Here and Heaven

Peter Graystone

CANTERBURY
PRESS
Norwich

**For my parents, John and Mary Graystone,
in whose home I unexpectedly found myself
sheltering when I wrote this book.**

© Peter Graystone 2006

First published in 2006 by the Canterbury Press Norwich
(a publishing imprint of Hymns Ancient & Modern Limited,
a registered charity)
9–17 St Alban's Place, London N1 0NX

www.scm-canterburypress.co.uk

British Library Cataloguing in Publication data

A catalogue record for this book is available
from the British Library

ISBN 1-85311-720-X/978-1-85311-720-6

Typeset by Regent Typesetting, London
Printed and bound by Bookmarque Ltd, Croydon, Surrey

Contents

Here are all 99 things to do between here and Heaven. Tick the star as you achieve each one. If a friend or relative has done it too, write their name next to it.

1   Watch the sun rise ☆ . . . .

2   Bake bread ☆ . . . .

3   Read a Gospel in one sitting ☆ . . . .

4   Give blood ☆ . . . .

5   Examine an icon ☆ . . . .

6   Give your testimony ☆ . . . .

7   Learn a musical instrument ☆ . . . .

8   Find out about Judaism ☆ . . . .

9   Work an allotment ☆ . . . .

10   Go on a protest rally ☆ . . . .

11   Revisit your childhood self ☆ . . . .

12   Take part in a Tenebrae service ☆ . . . .

13   Bury a time capsule ☆ . . . .

14   Break a bad habit ☆ . . . .

15   Learn New Testament Greek ☆ . . . .

16   Milk a cow ☆ . . . .

17   Light a candle ☆ . . . .

18   Go on a retreat ☆ . . . .

19   Make a will ☆ . . . .

20   Visit an Orthodox service ☆ . . . .

21   Watch a birth ☆ . . . .

The 99

1 Watch the sun rise

HOW? Choose a vantage point where there is a good view of the horizon when you face east. Many places on the coast offer fine views eastwards over the sea, but you could equally choose a hilltop looking over a city or fields. Standing stones such as Stonehenge attract crowds to watch the sun rise at the summer solstice (21 June) because of an assumed connection with pre-Christian religious rituals. Since the middle of the 18th century, Christians have gathered on hilltops (originally cemeteries) in the early hours of Easter Sunday to praise the risen Jesus as the sun rises.

Use the internet to find out the time when the sun will rise (visit www.weather.co.uk, enter the location, and click 'Climate'). Be at the site an hour before that in order to appreciate the depth of darkness of the night, and the changing colours and shades following the dawn. Wear warm clothes.

HOW EXTREME?

Here → ① ❷ ③ ④ ⑤ → Heaven

What should I expect?

During a sunrise you may find yourself reflecting on the goodness of God the creator, who has made the planet both complex and beautiful. The spectacular colours are due to an effect called Rayleigh scattering. Particles in our atmosphere cause the light of the sun, which is constantly white, to split into its component colours. The most common particles, oxygen and nitrogen, cause the light to be scattered at the frequency that we observe as being in the blue spectrum, so the sky appears blue when the sun is overhead. During sunrise, the distance the light travels to our eyes is greater, so the blue light is more scattered. As a result, more of the light from the red and orange spectrum reaches our eyes, sometimes with a dazzling impact.

Thank God that the display is constant and commonplace, but is also magnificent and full of wonder – adjectives that could also describe him. The very same effect was observed by Jesus, by Abraham, and by prehistoric humans. God has been faithful and gracious to his creation through all that time, as the earth has spun on its orbit of the sun. Our increased understanding of how it happens has only led to a greater awe of the God who imagined it into being.

How much?

💰 Nothing, but it is worth the expense of travelling to a beautiful location.

🕐 50 minutes. Or eight hours and fifty minutes if you stay up all night waiting.

2

Don't!

Don't be disappointed if an overcast sky means the colours are mainly grey. Clouds too are a wonder of God's creation.

 ## Who says?

Praised be you, my Lord, with all your creatures, especially Sir Brother Sun, who is the day and through whom you give us light. And he is beautiful and radiant with great splendours, and bears likeness of you, Most High One.
Francis of Assisi, founder of the Franciscan order, 1182–1226

 ## You are most likely to think

To have a God with the ability to create a world in which life is possible is wonderful; to have a God with the imagination to fill it with such beauty is stupendous.

 ## You are least likely to think

The display in front of me is the result of the defraction of light through the haphazard weather as the planet turns on its axis in this godless universe.

To help you reflect

Come, let us return to the Lord.
He has torn us to pieces but he will heal us;
he has injured us but he will bind up our wounds.
Let us press on to acknowledge him . . .
As surely as the sun rises, he will appear;
he will come to us like the winter rains,
like the spring rains that water the earth.
Hosea 6.1, 3

[Give the Lord's] people the knowledge of salvation
through the forgiveness of their sins,
because of the tender mercy of our God,
by which the rising sun will come to us from heaven
to shine on those living in darkness
and in the shadow of death,
to guide our feet into the path of peace.
Luke 1.77–79

The date I saw the sun rise

Where, and who else was there?

The colours I saw

What I will remember between here and heaven

3

2 Bake bread

HOW? Sprinkle 15g dried yeast on to 450ml warm water and stir in a teaspoon of sugar. Leave the mixture in a warm place for ten minutes. Meanwhile, sieve 675g plain wholemeal flour and two teaspoons of salt into a bowl and rub in 15g margarine. Add the yeast liquid, now frothy, and mix it into dough.

Shake flour on to a flat surface, put the dough on it, and knead it for ten minutes until it is smooth and stretchy. Rub some oil around a large bowl, put the dough into it, and cover it with cling film. Leave it for about two hours and come back to it when it has doubled in size (in a warm place one hour will be sufficient). Put it back on a floured surface, flatten it to knock any air bubbles out, and knead it for another five minutes as the dough gets firmer.

Divide the dough into about 18 pieces and roll each one into a ball. Rub margarine over the surface of baking trays, and place the rolls on them, about 3cm apart. Loosely cover this with cling film and leave it in a warm place again, this time for an hour. Meanwhile, heat the oven to 230° or gas mark 8. When the dough has grown again, put the rolls in the oven for 15–20 minutes. To test whether they are cooked, tap the rolls on the bottom – they should be firm and sound hollow. Put them on a wire tray to cool. Then share them.

HOW EXTREME?

Here → ① ❷ ③ ④ ⑤ → Heaven

What should I expect?

People find baking bread a surprisingly spiritual experience. Because the ingredients transform, grow, rest and give great pleasure, the process may lead you to reflect on the goodness of God's creation – abundance, fertility, change. The act of making bread slows you down, and as your speed decreases, your thinking increases. In fact, the actual time you spend in contact with the bread is not great and the process is much simpler than some assume, but the kneading requires patience, and the yeast works its everyday miracle at a pace that cannot be rushed.

Shared with others, newly-baked bread has echoes of communion. It is not by accident that Jesus asked to be remembered by shared bread – an ancient, worldwide food formed out of the simplest ingredients. Like him, it is life-giving. In the Bible it is a symbol of humankind's most basic needs, both physical and spiritual. So there is something timeless and satisfying in creating and sharing it, whether you thump more anger or love into the kneading.

How much?

 About £1 for 18 rolls.

 Three and a half hours, during most of which you can do something else.

4

Don't!

Don't feel you have had the same experience if you use a bread-making machine. You need to sink your hands in the dough.

You are most likely to think

Ah! That smell! Give me another!

You are least likely to think

This is the best thing since sliced bread.

Who says?

The time I spend baking bread has become a time for me to see the beauty and hope in chaos. When I bake, I am certain to make a mess, to have flour up to my elbows, and dough turning to paste on the hairs of my arms. Yet baking is also about precision – the grammes and ounces that keep me grounded. Baking a loaf of bread is esoteric and mundane. It is divine and it is earthy. It is eternal, and it will turn to dust.
Alice Downs, priest and cook, writing in Leaven for our Lives

To help you reflect

He who supplies seed to the sower and bread for food will also supply and increase your store of seed and will enlarge the harvest of your righteousness.
2 Corinthians 9.10

[Jesus] told them still another parable: 'The kingdom of heaven is like yeast that a woman took and mixed into a large amount of flour until it worked all through the dough.'
Matthew 13.33

The date I baked bread

The people I shared the bread with

The comments they made

What I will remember between here and heaven

3 Read a Gospel in one sitting

HOW? Curl up in an armchair and open a Bible as if you were opening a novel. Choose Mark's Gospel because it is the shortest. Surround yourself with chocolate, drinks, or whatever would usually accompany an evening's entertainment. Try to pretend that you don't know how it ends.

HOW EXTREME?

Here → **❶** ② ③ ④ ⑤ → Heaven

What should I expect?

This is the story of the life of Jesus read in the way it was intended to be read. The chapters and verses that divide up the text were introduced in the 13th and 16th centuries respectively. The Gospel writers first presented their work as seamless and searing stories of three years in the life of someone whom they admired beyond measure. Two of them (Matthew and Luke) also provided a prologue by researching Jesus' birth.

For 30 years after Jesus' resurrection almost nothing was written down about his life, because most of the eye-witnesses were illiterate, and because they expected Jesus to return to earth in person any day. Stories were passed on by word of mouth. It was only as a generation of children grew up who had not met Jesus that the need for a written record became apparent. Many accounts were written, some of which can still be read even though they are not in the Bible. As you would expect of stories that were passed from person to person, some had wild exaggerations. There was a serious job of research and clarification to be done, drawing together the information and sorting fact from fantasy. By AD 150, four accounts had emerged as reliable.

Mark's Gospel is full of action, racing through Jesus' life. Matthew based his account on Mark's, expanding it to explain how Jesus fulfilled all that the Old Testament anticipated. Luke is more of a teacher, also enlarging Mark's account to stress the salvation that Jesus had brought. John, writing later, goes deeper in explaining how Jesus' life and teaching reveal God.

How much?

£ A basic edition of the Bible costs between £7 and £15. An individual Gospel costs about £5. Or you can read any of the Gospels free online at www.rejesus.co.uk

Mark's Gospel will take about 90 minutes to read. For Matthew or Luke, allow about three hours – you will need a break in the middle. John, although it is not so long, will probably also take three hours because the ideas are complicated.

Don't!

Don't break your reading up into little sections, as daily Bible reading schemes tend to. Instead, take in the entire, compelling sweep of his life in its excitement, tragedy and triumph.

 Who says?

I got the deepest feeling [that the whole material was extraordinarily alive]. My work changed me. I came to the conclusion that these words bear the seal of the Son of Man and God. They are the Magna Carta of the human spirit.
E. V. Rieu, translator of the four Gospels, 1887–1972

 You are most likely to think

Such a burning compassion. Such a loving mind. Such a technicolour imagination. Such a strong will. Such a rebellious nature. Such a sacrificial life.

 You are least likely to think

Just as I remember from a child's first book of Bible stories – worthy, saintly and bland.

To help you reflect

Many have undertaken to draw up an account of the things that have been fulfilled among us, just as they were handed down to us by those who from the first were eyewitnesses and servants of the word. Therefore, since I myself have carefully investigated everything from the beginning, it seemed good also to me to write an orderly account for you, most excellent Theophilus, so that you may know the certainty of the things you have been taught.
Luke 1.1–4

Jesus did many other miraculous signs in the presence of his disciples, which are not recorded in this book. But these are written that you may believe that Jesus is the Christ, the Son of God, and that by believing you may have life in his name.
John 20.30, 31

The date I read a complete Gospel

Which one?

Something I noticed about Jesus that I had not recognized before

What I will remember between here and heaven

4 Give blood

HOW? Mobile units regularly visit towns the length and breadth of the UK. To find out the nearest venue and time, visit www.blood.co.uk (England), www.welsh-blood.co.uk/English (Wales), www.scotblood.co.uk (Scotland) or www.nibts.org (Northern Ireland). It is possible to enrol online, but you don't need to. Just turn up!

HOW EXTREME?

Here → ① ❷ ③ ④ ⑤ → Heaven

What should I expect?

A nurse will ask you some questions and invite you to fill in a form. He or she will then take one drop of blood from the end of your finger, which will be tested to check that you are well enough to donate blood, and to identify your blood type. You then lie on a couch, while the nurse slides a needle painlessly into a vein in your arm. For about ten minutes you chat while a pint of blood is taken. The needle is then removed, and you will be invited to sit and have refreshments so that you spend a few minutes at a slower pace instead of rushing away. You will get a card that thanks you and invites you to return four months later. Your body will replace the quantity of blood within a day and its richness within a week.

This is an immensely practical way of showing the love for our fellow human beings that Jesus selected as one of the two most important commandments. Bringing healing has always been a sign that the Kingdom of God is present, so you can expect to feel that you have joined Jesus in the task of doing God's work in the world. Enjoy the fact that giving blood is an act of generosity, and that (unlike some countries) there is no payment to change it into merely a commercial transaction.

With their limited scientific knowledge, the writers of the Old Testament believed that the blood contained all the substances that made the difference between a person being alive and dead. This led to them treating blood with great honour, particularly in the sacrifice of animals. Some unorthodox religious groups (such as Jehovah's Witnesses) interpret this as forbidding blood transfusions. However, for most Christians it serves to make their donation, which will preserve someone else's life, seem an even more precious gift.

How much?

 Free, and they will give you a cup of tea and a biscuit.

 One hour at most.

8

Don't!

Don't donate blood if you are under 17 or over 60, if you are pregnant or ill (the websites are more specific). And don't put others at risk by donating blood if, during the past year, you have visited a country where malaria is common, or had a tattoo or body piercing.

 ## Who says?

I've been thinking about this for a long time. Something for the benefit of the country as a whole. What should it be, I thought: become a blood donor or join the Young Conservatives? Anyway, as I'm not looking for a wife and I can't play table tennis, here I am.
Tony Hancock, in the television situation comedy The Blood Donor, *by Ray Galton and Alan Simpson*

 ## You are most likely to think

Is that all there is to it?

 ## You are least likely to think

I hope my blood goes to someone I approve of.

To help you reflect

David praised the Lord ... 'Who am I, and who are my people, that we should be able to give as generously as this? Everything comes from you, and we have given only what comes from your hand.'
1 Chronicles 29.14

You will be made rich in every way so that you can be generous on every occasion, and through us your generosity will result in thanksgiving to God. This service that you perform is not only supplying the needs of God's people but is also overflowing in many expressions of thanks to God.
2 Corinthians 9.11–12

	The date I donated my blood

	Where?

	These were my thoughts as it happened

	What I will remember between here and heaven

5 Examine an icon

HOW? There are three ways to examine icons – by participating in an act of worship at an Orthodox church, by visiting an art gallery, or by looking at pictures in a book or on the internet.

In Orthodox practice, icons are provided to be worshipped (which is distinct from being adored, as only God can be). An icon is more than a religious painting. It is created as an act of prayer to precise specifications, using techniques and materials in a way that has not changed for centuries. Opening yourself to God in the presence of an icon is a way of encountering, in a sense, the actual presence of the subject that has been painted, so doing this in a church as part of an act of worship is by far the most valuable way.

Icons are also collected in art galleries. In the UK, the finest museum specializing in icons is the Temple Gallery in London which also displays works of art online (www.templegallery.com). In a gallery it is, however, easier to focus on the beauty of the artworks than it is to unlock their spiritual impact.

To look at a photograph of an icon in a book or to purchase a replica shows what it looks like, but is not ideal for use in prayer. Worship requires being in the presence of the object (especially if it incorporates a relic of a saint, such as a bone).

HOW EXTREME?

Here → ① **❷** ③ ④ ⑤ → Heaven

What should I expect?

Stand in front of the icon, relax and invite God to speak to you through it. Notice the way that inverse perspective is used so that objects that are close are painted smaller than those that are far away. The effect of this is to draw you into the picture, as if you are not only looking at the surface, but through it into the reality beyond. Look at the face portrayed, and ask yourself what mood it is inviting worshippers to assume. All the other elements of the painting (clothes, objects, colours, poses) have been put there deliberately. Why? Can the icon teach you about your place in the world? Can it point you to God, or challenge you to emulate the subject?

How much?

💰 Travel to and from the church or gallery. (For more information about visiting Orthodox churches, turn to the 20th thing to do between here and heaven.)

🕐 Examining an icon requires more time than looking at a painting. Dwell calmly on each image for three minutes or more.

Don't!

Don't rush.

 Who says?

Icons are a true mirror of the divine. They are a window into heaven. What I love is the stillness of them; the fact that we venerate them as if they were real presences. They have a quality that does not demand anything of you. They are there, saying, 'Take me if you want.' They are a vessel through which the Holy Spirit might be able to talk.
John Tavener, composer

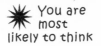 **You are most likely to think**

What I can see is beautiful, but there are things that God has put in this world that are real, but which I cannot see. In time, I want to appreciate that they are beautiful too.

 You are least likely to think

Mickey Mouse is an icon too. I wonder which will have a more lasting impact on me.

To help you reflect

The Lord has chosen Bezalel son of Uri, the son of Hur, of the tribe of Judah, and he has filled him with the Spirit of God, with skill, ability and knowledge in all kinds of crafts – to make artistic designs for work in gold, silver and bronze, to cut and set stones, to work in wood and to engage in all kinds of artistic craftsmanship . . . just as the Lord has commanded.
Exodus 35.30—36.1

This is what I seek:
that I may dwell in the house of the Lord
* all the days of my life,*
to gaze upon the beauty of the Lord
and to seek him in his temple.
Psalm 27.4

The date I spent time in front of an icon

What was the subject portrayed?

Details and truths of which I became aware

What I will remember between here and heaven

6 Give your testimony

HOW? Your testimony is the true story of the difference that God has made to your life. Telling other people this story, having thought in advance about what you are going to say, can bring great encouragement to fellow-Christians, and can show people who do not have an active faith that following Jesus is normal, rewarding and worth considering for themselves. Ask a church leader whether a suitable occasion might arise publicly to tell the story of how you have come to put your faith in God. He or she may recommend giving your testimony to a small group connected with the church, or may suggest that it would be appropriate to tell your story during a church service.

To prepare your testimony, think about and write down the main reason that you are a follower of Jesus. Can you think when you first became aware of how important that reason is? Is there an anecdote attached, or was it a growing realization? Who or what helped you understand? What differences are you aware of in your lifestyle and priorities before and after your faith became real? Give as much interesting detail as you can, but don't exaggerate or make yourself seem like a hero.

You don't have to tell your entire life story, or say everything that is significant to you as a Christian. You could give a testimony about just one thing that has happened to you (for example, about how being made redundant shook your trust in God but didn't end it, or about how the birth of a grandson made you think about what kind of world you want him to grow up in). Save the rest of your life story as a treat for another occasion. There is no rule that dictates what your testimony must be like, but it should definitely encourage your listeners by showing that trust in Jesus has had a positive impact on your life.

HOW EXTREME?

Here → ① ❷ ③ ④ ⑤ → Heaven

What should I expect?

People are fascinated by stories like these because, unlike a sermon that is slick and abstract, a testimony is a real account of struggle and hope. It doesn't explain what happens in theory; it shows what takes place in reality.

To tell the story of your life 'warts and all' makes you very vulnerable. Once you have been honest, you can never make something secret again. However, it is that vulnerability that people find so compelling. It helps them realize that the difficulties they experience in believing in or obeying God are not unique to them. It gives them confidence to trust him. So expect to be warmly thanked for sharing your story, and to feel that you have done more to introduce people to all that Jesus can do for them than a library full of books could.

Don't!

Don't use Christian jargon like 'born again' or 'converted', which has no meaning to people who are not used to going to church. Find ways of explaining what those things mean in practice.

 You are most likely to think

They must all think what a great God I follow.

 You are least likely to think

They must all think what a great person I am.

 Who says?

What other people think of me is becoming less and less important; what they think of Jesus because of me is critical.
Cliff Richard, singer

H o w   m u c h ?

💰 Nothing

🕐 Four to five minutes is a good length of time in which to tell a story and keep people's interest. If you are reading from a written script, that will be 750 words.

To help you reflect

Always be prepared to give an answer to everyone who asks you to give the reason for the hope that you have. But do this with gentleness and respect, keeping a clear conscience, so that those who speak maliciously against your good behaviour in Christ may be ashamed of their slander.
1 Peter 3.15, 16

We are Christ's ambassadors, as though God were making his appeal through us. We implore you on Christ's behalf: Be reconciled to God.
2 Corinthians 5.20

	The date I gave my testimony
🖩	

	What was the setting?
◇?	

	The most important thing I said
📝	

	What I will remember between here and heaven
🌲	

7 Learn a musical instrument

HOW? Choose the instrument that you would like to learn for social reasons (because playing drums in a band or cello in an orchestra is creatively rewarding), for practical reasons (because a guitar fits better in the lift to a tenth floor flat than a piano), or simply because you fancy it (a harp sounds gorgeous anywhere).

If you have left school, the most reliable way to find a teacher is by word of mouth. Other ways of making contact are through the lists that most music shops keep, or via www.musicteachers.co.uk.

Valuable advice for beginners can be found at www.paythepiper.co.uk. Music exams (grades 1 to 8) can give you an incentive, but there is no substitute for putting in regular practice, and most adults take up music because they want to play, not because they need another qualification.

HOW EXTREME?

Here → ① ② ③ ❹ ⑤ → Heaven

What should I expect?

All civilizations of history have used music to lead them beyond the everyday toward the divine. Christianity, and before that Judaism, have particularly embraced music as a means of worshipping God and seen musical talent as a gift that he alone can give. This is true whenever music is made, not just when it is used in the context of church worship.

Of course, instruments can be used for music in a way that diverts people's attention from God (which is why the Puritans decided in the 17th century to ban them and praise God with voices alone). However, by being a person who creates, rather than just consumes, music, you become part of an activity that touches people in a way that neither thoughts nor words alone could. You are at the heart of something that communicates insights beyond materialism and puts people in touch with deep spiritual values. More than a personal achievement, more than a lasting joy, more than shared pleasure, you are showing why you are in the image of God. You are becoming creative, like your Creator.

How much?

£18 to £20 per lesson is a typical price, but expert teachers charge more. The price of basic instruments varies from £200 for a violin, through £400 for a flute, to £3,000 for a bassoon. Consider hiring an instrument from a music shop while you are making up your mind, at about £15 per month for a clarinet or trumpet.

Music lessons usually last 30 minutes. However, the teacher cannot learn the instrument for you, and you will need to practise. Fifteen minutes every day is recommended for a beginner who seriously wants to learn. As you get better, doubling that becomes necessary, but also more enjoyable.

Don't!

Don't attempt to use 'teach yourself' books and manage without a teacher unless you are naturally gifted and determined. (Drums and guitars are possible exceptions.)

 ## Who says?

A most wonderful and glorious gift of God, which has the power to drive out Satan and to fend off temptations and evil thoughts.
Martin Luther, German theologian and reformer, 1485–1546

 ## You are most likely to think

Mozart, Mendelssohn, Mahler, me – we have one thing in common.

 ## You are least likely to think

Mozart, Mendelssohn, Mahler, me – we have many things in common.

To help you reflect

*It is good to praise the Lord
and make music to your name, O Most High,
to proclaim your love in the morning
and your faithfulness at night,
to the music of the ten-stringed lyre
and the melody of the harp.
For you make me glad by your deeds, O Lord;
I sing for joy at the works of your hands.
Psalm 92.1–4*

*[David selected performers who] were under the supervision of their fathers for the music of the temple of the Lord, with cymbals, lyres and harps, for the ministry at the house of God . . . Along with their relatives – all of them trained and skilled in music for the Lord – they numbered 288, young and old alike.
1 Chronicles 25.5–8*

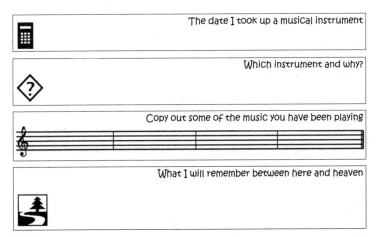

The date I took up a musical instrument

Which instrument and why?

Copy out some of the music you have been playing

What I will remember between here and heaven

8 Find out about Judaism

HOW? Judaism 101 has a fine website dedicated to helping non-Jews understand the beliefs, practices and history of the Jews. At its online encyclopaedia, you can choose to read basic, intermediate or advanced information. Visit www.jewfaq.org and click 'Table of contents'.

Helpful books include *Judaism, a Very Short Introduction* (Norman Solomon, Oxford Paperbacks) and *Jewish Spirituality: A Brief Introduction for Christians* (Lawrence Kushner, Jewish Lights Publishing).

The Jewish Museum, on two sites in North London, is an outstanding collection, although stronger on the history and art of Judaism than its beliefs. It is open from 10.00 to 16.00, but closed on Fridays and Saturdays (www.jewishmuseum.org.uk). Many synagogues welcome visitors but anxieties about security have led them to insist that you make contact in advance and bring identification. Addresses can be found at www.somethingjewish.co.uk (the 'UK synagogues' hotspot is on the left). For a group of 15–30 adults, the Board of Deputies of British Jews can organize a day of customized activities that introduces Jewish food, worship and education in an experiential way (at www.bod.org.uk, click 'Seeing Jewish life tours' on the right).

HOW EXTREME?

Here → ① ② ❸ ④ ⑤ → Heaven

What should I expect?

Expect to discover a community in which some practise their religion faithfully while others are secular, but strongly regard themselves as part of a people with a unique identity. Core beliefs are that there is one, all-powerful God who created the universe and has a unique relationship with the Jewish people. Devout Jews long for the coming of the Messiah, God's anointed one, who will inaugurate an era of peace. (Christians believe Jesus to have fulfilled this.)

Day-to-day life for sincere Jewish people is shaped by the laws and traditions of the community, rooted in the Torah (the first five books of the Bible) and other writings. Many Jewish obligations arise from these – acts of worship in the home and the synagogue on the Sabbath (Friday evening to Saturday evening), circumcision for males, festivals recalling historical events, and avoidance of certain foods. Jewish practice has been repeatedly refined to respond to their need to survive persecution, from their exile in Babylon in the 6th century BC to the Holocaust of the 20th century.

Don't!

Don't make the mistake of assuming that the word 'Israel' in the Bible refers to the present-day secular state of Israel. To do so without taking into account what God has done over two thousand subsequent years has led to some Christians lending their support to actions that have caused suffering in the Middle East.

Both books cost £6.99. Admission to the Jewish Museum costs £3.50 (Campden site) and £2 (Finchley site), with concessions. A 'Seeing Jewish Life' tour costs £15 per head.

The books listed can each be read in two evenings, and exploring Judaism 101 will take a similar length of time. Allow most of a day for the museums or the tour.

H o w   m u c h ?

 Who says?

If something is hateful to you, do not do it to your neighbour. This is the whole of the Jewish law. The rest is merely commentary. Go and study it!
Hillel the Elder, Jewish theologian about 70BC–AD10

 You are most likely to think

These are the deep and precious roots of my Christian faith.

 You are least likely to think

Jesus was a Christian.

To help you reflect

Consider Abraham: 'He believed God, and it was credited to him as righteousness.' Understand, then, that those who believe are children of Abraham. The Scripture foresaw that God would justify the Gentiles by faith, and announced the gospel in advance to Abraham: 'All nations will be blessed through you.' So those who have faith are blessed along with Abraham, the man of faith.
Galatians 3.6–9

I will tell of the kindnesses of the Lord,
the deeds for which he is to be praised,
according to all the Lord has done for us –
yes, the many good things he has done for the
house of Israel,
according to his compassion and many kindnesses.
He said, 'Surely they are my people,
children who will not be false to me';
and so he became their Saviour.
Isaiah 63.7, 8

	The date I found out about Judaism

	How?

	Something I learnt that changed me

	What I will remember between here and heaven

9 Work an allotment

HOW? Contact your local council to find out where the nearest allotments are. The council will allocate you a plot or (more likely) add your name to a waiting list. The average size is 250 square metres, but this can be daunting for a beginner, so half-plots are often available. The council will provide the land – which may be overgrown when you first set foot on it – a water supply, and secure surrounds to prevent vandalism. A few additionally have sheds, toilets, or composting facilities. Some sites are privately owned by local allotment associations.

The plot must mainly be used for growing fruit or vegetables, but some councils allow livestock, such as chickens, as well. You are only allowed to grow produce that will feed your family and friends, so you cannot use the plot to start a business. The 'About renting and using a plot' section of www.allotments.org has good advice for beginners.

HOW EXTREME?

Here → ① ② ③ ④ **❺** → Heaven

What should I expect?

Owning an allotment puts you in control of the food you eat, which is important to those who want to be sure they are eating produce that is free of chemicals and has not been genetically modified. The taste of fresh food, and the knowledge that it was grown with your own hands, substantially increases the joy of eating it. Working the ground is excellent exercise, of course, and the exchange of advice between gardeners allows friendships to form effortlessly.

We live in a world where it is increasingly difficult to make a connection between the meals we eat and the circumstances in which the food was produced. A burger looks nothing like a cow! Even vegetables can be bought in a supermarket already washed, sliced and chopped. Producing your own food reminds you that the Creator God has put us in a world which teems with growth, but has given humans the responsibility of cultivating it in a responsible way. Working an allotment can reawaken your sense of wonder that a pumpkin the size of your head grows from a seed the size of your fingernail. The harder you work in order to eat, the more thankful you are. And the more thankful you are, the more content you become.

 Who says?

Gardening is an active participation in the deepest mysteries of the universe. By gardening, our children learn that they constitute with all growing things a single community of life.
Thomas Berry, theologian

You are most likely to think

No matter how good a carrot from a shop tastes, one that I grew myself tastes better.

You are least likely to think

I do miss the tang of added chemicals in my food.

Depending on the region, allotments are rented annually for between £37 and £53. There are often reductions (for instance, for senior citizens or half a plot). To buy enough new tools to start from scratch, allow £250–£300. Vegetable seeds cost £1.50–£2.50 per packet.

The time commitment depends on the size of the allotment. If you take on a vacant and overgrown plot in Autumn, allow five days to get 250 square metres into a workable condition. Subsequently, eight hours per week is a reasonable guide at the height of the season. Potatoes, parsnips or onions are low maintenance, but tomatoes require a lot of attention.

Don't!

Don't take on more than you can sustain. For a less extreme version, see 'Grow something you eat', which is the 25th thing to do between here and heaven.

To help you reflect

[God] has not left himself without testimony. He has shown kindness by giving you rain from heaven and crops in their seasons; he provides you with plenty of food and fills your hearts with joy.
Acts 14.17

Make it your ambition to lead a quiet life, to mind your own business and to work with your hands, just as we told you, so that your daily life may win the respect of outsiders and so that you will not be dependent on anybody.
1 Thessalonians 4.11, 12

The date I began to work an allotment

What I grew in the first season

My first meal with home-grown vegetables

What I will remember between here and heaven

10 Go on a protest rally

HOW? Causes that attract Christians to campaign in large numbers are those that uphold the values of the Kingdom of God. When they are moved to take to the streets, it is on behalf of poor people who are denied justice, oppressed people who need release, or war-scarred people who seek peace. Rallies that are worth supporting are well organized and have a specific message to communicate to those with the power to bring change.

Visit the website of the organization that is planning the rally. Make sure you know and understand its objective. (If it is unclear, the event is probably not worth supporting.) Find out the time and place, and make sure that there is a map that shows the route of any march that is planned, and the location of performances and speeches. Satisfy yourself that care has been taken over the safety of the event (for instance, the provision of toilets, facilities for disabled people, first aid and stewards). Well in advance, investigate travel and accommodation, so that there is no danger of you getting stranded unexpectedly. As with any event that involves being in a large crowd, take appropriate clothes and shoes for the weather that is expected, and carry food and water.

Take something with you that shows what cause you are supporting (a placard or T-shirt, for instance), and join in enthusiastically and noisily.

HOW EXTREME?

Here → ① ② ❸ ④ ⑤ → Heaven

What should I expect?

The irony of protest rallies that support the values of the Kingdom of God is that although the cause is concerned with tragedy, the event is usually exhilarating. It is uplifting to join large numbers of Christians who are committed to taking action on behalf of suffering people. And discovering a common cause with people of other faiths or no faith expands your understanding of the vast scale on which God is working in his Kingdom.

Expect speeches that clarify the importance of opposing evil, and joyful music that allows your heart to be as excited about addressing injustice as your head. Seek out acts of worship (always present, but sometimes hard to find) that allow you to pray quietly and seriously amongst the clamour. Many rallies include a march (more often a saunter) that makes your act of Christian witness public. Official marches have always arranged the co-operation of the police in advance, and are safe and peaceful.

Travel expenses to and from the event, and accommodation if you intend to be away from home overnight.

 Most large-scale events require the investment of a whole day.

Don't!

Don't defy a policeman, damage anyone's property, behave in a way that will bring the good cause you are supporting into disrepute, or do anything else likely to lead to your arrest.

 Who says?

To sin by silence when they should protest makes cowards out of men.
Abraham Lincoln, president of the USA, 1809–1865

 You are most likely to think

In the New Testament, James tells us that faith without actions is dead. Today my faith really is alive and making a difference to the world.

You are least likely to think

I really should have stayed home and kept up to date with the soaps.

To help you reflect

[Jeremiah protested:] 'Whenever I speak, I cry out proclaiming violence and destruction. So the word of the Lord has brought me insult and reproach all day long. But if I say, "I will not mention him or speak any more in his name," his word is in my heart like a fire, a fire shut up in my bones. I am weary of holding it in; indeed, I cannot.'
Jeremiah 20.8, 9

[Approaching Jerusalem], the whole crowd of disciples began joyfully to praise God in loud voices . . . Some of the Pharisees in the crowd said to Jesus, 'Teacher, rebuke your disciples!' 'I tell you,' he replied, 'if they keep quiet, the stones will cry out.' As he approached Jerusalem and saw the city, he wept over it.
Luke 19.37–41

	The date and place I attended a protest rally
	The just cause about which I was demonstrating
	What changed (in the world or in me) as a result of the demonstration?
	What I will remember between here and heaven

11 Revisit your childhood self

HOW? Find a comfortable place and prepare for a meditation. Unlike a daydream, you will guide what you think about, not just let random thoughts occur.

Imagine yourself in a beautiful, spacious place – one that you have actually visited and in which you have been happy. Walk through it alone. Enjoy the view. Think about the care with which God has created this place, and the way he fills every aspect of it. As you stroll, become aware of another figure in the far distance. The figure is too far away to identify, but it is a human. As it approaches, become conscious that the person is the same gender as you, although much younger. It is a young child. Walk on, until you are close enough to identify features. It is you.

Draw near and greet your childhood self. Remind yourself what life was like at that age. Then, taking stock of all that has happened to you subsequently, tell your childhood self the things you would like him or her to know about what lies ahead, and how to be prepared for them. Take time over this. In your imagination, give an expression of affection to the child in the way you would most like to have been loved when you were that age. Turn around, walk away, and bring yourself back to the realities of the room you are in.

HOW EXTREME?

Here → **①** ② ③ ④ ⑤ → Heaven

What should I expect?

You are the same person that you were as a child, and things that happened then have shaped the way you are today. The child that you once were can be spiritual, playful and spontaneous, but he or she can also be fearful and critical. Knowing that can help you understand why you are attracted to certain people, or react in particular ways. It can reveal the logic of what makes you scared, angry or lonely. When you know that, you can benefit from it, or control it so that it does not trap you.

Throughout this meditation, keep the presence of God closely in your thoughts. You are not attempting to heal yourself; you are opening an opportunity for God (and God alone) to heal you. The least you can expect is some interesting memories; the most you can expect is for God to develop a more wise, liberated and loving you.

How much?

 Nothing.

 Perhaps 30 minutes to meditate, but it may take a long time to work through the implications.

Don't!

Don't reopen distressing memories unless you are in a position to deal with the feelings. If you are seeking to heal deep wounds you need the guidance of someone experienced. To find help, contact the Association of Christian Counsellors at www.doveuk.com/acc and click on 'Find a counsellor'.

 Who says?

The wild rose can only be a wild rose, a thistle can only be a thistle; to people only God gave the power to change their ways.
Catherine Bramwell Booth, Salvation Army commissioner, 1883–1987

 You are most likely to think

I need not be imprisoned. In God there is healing.

 You are least likely to think

What a horrible little brat!

To help you reflect

When I was a child, I talked like a child, I thought like a child, I reasoned like a child. When I became an adult, I put childish ways behind me. Now we see but a poor reflection as in a mirror; then we shall see face to face. Now I know in part; then I shall know fully, even as I am fully known. And now these three remain: faith, hope and love. But the greatest of these is love.
1 Corinthians 13.11–13

When I was a boy in my father's house, still tender, and an only child of my mother, he taught me and said, 'Lay hold of my words with all your heart; keep my commands and you will live . . . Do not forsake wisdom, and she will protect you; love her, and she will watch over you.'
Proverbs 4.3–6

The date I revisited my childhood self

What advice would the mature me give to the child I was?

What changes might I make?

What I will remember between here and heaven

12 Take part in a Tenebrae service

HOW? Tenebrae means shadows. It is an evening service that takes place on one of the days immediately before Easter, using darkness as a way of focusing your mind on the horror of Jesus' crucifixion. You will need to look quite hard to find a church that offers it. Telephone the offices of nearby Roman Catholic churches, or 'high' Anglican churches (the kinds that have a great love of ritual) and ask whether they know of local churches which have a Tenebrae service on Good Friday or Easter Eve.

HOW EXTREME?

Here → ① **❷** ③ ④ ⑤ → Heaven

What should I expect?

This is an unremittingly solemn service that allows you to enter into the emotions surrounding the crucifixion of Jesus. There is no happy ending. It leaves you in a darkness and despair that will not be relieved until Easter morning dawns.

The service begins with the church laid out in its usual way. Eight candles are alight. There is a hymn that uses all the musical resources of the church, and then a Bible reading that begins to tell the story of how and why Jesus died. The reader blows out one of the candles. As the service continues, the church and the style of worship become increasingly bare. Seven readings follow, after each of which a candle is blown out and the amount of light in the church is decreased. Progressively, decorations are taken away or covered until the room is stripped of banners, crosses, or anything beautiful. The musical styles become plainer, with the choir walking out, not to return, and then the musicians, so that the final hymn is unaccompanied.

Finally, the leader of the service reads from Psalm 22 words that Jesus screamed when he was on the cross: 'My God, my God, why have you forsaken me?' The final candle is extinguished, leaving the church in absolute darkness. A mighty crash, such as the slamming of a door, follows to represent the thud of the stone rolling across the entrance of the tomb. The people leave without a sound.

You will find this one of the most moving services of the year. Because it is unremittingly bleak, without a hint of resurrection, it will remind you that the first followers of Jesus witnessed his death without the advantage we have of knowing that new life was to follow. The style of the service acknowledges that suffering is a reality of existence for every human because it is a reality for God. Only by dwelling on the awfulness of Jesus' anguish is it possible fully to experience the joy of Easter morning.

Don't!

Don't talk to anyone as you leave the service. Go to bed with the darkness and wretchedness vivid in your mind.

You are most likely to think

I have had a glimpse at the utter desolation of a world in which God has died.

You are least likely to think

Christian worship is all froth and jollity.

How much?

£ Nothing.

🕐 50 to 60 minutes.

Who says?

Good Captain, maker of the light,
Who dost divide the day and night,
The sun is drowned beneath the sea,
Chaos is on us horribly:
O Christ, give back to faithful souls the light.
Prudentius, Spanish poet, in a prayer for Easter Eve, 348–410

To help you reflect

Jesus said to the chief priests, the officers of the temple guard, and the elders, who had come for him . . . 'Every day I was with you in the temple courts, and you did not lay a hand on me. But this is your hour – when darkness reigns.' Then seizing him, they led him away and took him into the house of the high priest.
Luke 22.52–54

Those crucified with [Jesus] heaped insults on him. At the sixth hour darkness came over the whole land until the ninth hour. And at the ninth hour Jesus cried out in a loud voice, 'Eloi, Eloi, lama sabachthani?' – which means, 'My God, my God, why have you forsaken me?' . . . With a loud cry, Jesus breathed his last.
Mark 15.32–34, 37

The date I attended a Tenebrae service

Where?

What happened that was unlike a usual service?

What I will remember between here and heaven

25

13 Bury a time capsule

HOW? The first modern attempt to preserve objects for a future generation was in 1939 at the New York World's Fair. Seeds, a doll, newsreel, a microscope and statistical information are buried under Flushing Meadow awaiting 6939.

You could create a small time capsule with children for them to open in their old age. Choose objects that are of personal interest, such as photographs, toys and letters. Alternatively, involve a community group in creating a capsule for a century hence, which contains objects that are representative of today's culture. Exclude objects containing rubber, wool, PVC, or anything edible unless you package them in such a way as to stop them giving off gas and causing other items to perish. If you choose something operated by electricity, leave details of the technology required, because the hardware will become a museum piece. Include a list of the contents, their colour and significance, and keep another copy in a safe place.

Hold a 'sealing ceremony' and place the capsule in a dark, dry place. Appoint an archivist whose responsibility is passing on the location to the next generation. Register what you have done with the International Time Capsule Society (click on 'About OU' at www.oglethorpe.edu).

HOW EXTREME?

Here → ① ② ❸ ④ ⑤ → Heaven

What should I expect?

A time capsule focuses your mind on what is important about today's culture by prompting you to imagine life in the future. Select items that will demonstrate to a future age what is good and beautiful about this decade, as well as cheap objects that give a sense of everyday life. Identify things in your home that would have astonished 19th-century ancestors, and take ideas from them. As you do so, register the many ways in which the world has got better over the last century and thank God for them. Cynicism about a world going to the dogs will become impossible. And you will find energy for passing on the good news of Jesus to the next generation, knowing that his presence will enrich the lives of your descendants in as real a way as he has yours.

How much?

 A time capsule made of acrylic polymers (longer lasting than metal containers) costs from £30 to £50, depending on size. Specialist conservation packaging and acid-free papers at various prices can be purchased at www.conservation-by-design.co.uk

 100 years and six hours.

26

Don't!

Don't bury it in the ground, where damp will ruin the contents and you are likely to forget it.

Who says?

We are blessing everything to be put into the time capsule on 29 December 2003. We have built the Kingdom of God on the foundation laid by those who preceded us. You in your day are a continuation of the journey through time of the people of God in this part of the world, all living, working and praising God for his glory. We pray that we will one day meet in the eternal life won for us by our Lord Jesus Christ.
John Steinbock, Bishop of Fresno, California, in a letter to his successor who in 2103 will open the capsule buried on the occasion of the centenary of St John's Cathedral

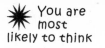

You are most likely to think

I hope that the people who open this live in a good and safe world, and have put their faith in Jesus Christ.

You are least likely to think

Nothing changes.

To help you reflect

Let this be written for a future generation,
that a people not yet created may praise the Lord . . .
'In the beginning you laid the foundations of the earth,
and the heavens are the work of your hands.
They will perish, but you remain;
they will all wear out like a garment.
Like clothing you will change them and they will be discarded.
But you remain the same, and your years will never end.'
Psalm 102.18, 25–27

All things are yours, whether . . . the world or life or death or the present or the future – all are yours, and you are of Christ, and Christ is of God.
1 Corinthians 3.21–23

	The date I buried a time capsule

	Its location and the date I anticipate it will be opened

	The objects I have put in it

	What I will remember between here and heaven

14 Break a bad habit

HOW? Begin by keeping track of the behaviour that has become habitual. Keep a diary so that you know what prompts it. For instance, what triggers you biting your nails or chewing your cheek? Is there a pattern to the occasions when you feel an urge to smoke a cigarette or access an internet site that is doing you no good? As your awareness of this increases, analyse what your feelings are as you succumb to the habit. What in your life is the habit addressing? Is it perhaps boredom, anger, stress, loneliness, anxiety?

Think of something you could do that is a more positive way of dealing with those feelings than the way that has become your automatic response. For example, massaging your palm instead of biting your nails, eating a piece of fruit instead of smoking (one that requires two hands to peel or prepare it), an online chess game instead of an online chatroom. Try to catch yourself indulging in the behaviour you want to change, and immediately substitute the alternative. Practise your new behaviour in the hope that it will become habitual too. Tell everyone you know what you are doing and what they can do to help you.

HOW EXTREME?

Here → ① ② ③ ❹ ⑤ → Heaven

What should I expect?

There are some cravings that God has built into the way he created us, for example, needing water, sleep or a loving touch. These are almost invariably life-enhancing. But there are other cravings that are artificial or adopted, and these can become destructive habits – eating until you are uncomfortably full, smoking or hurting yourself (even in minor ways like pulling hairs out). You do not have to do these things. But the only way to stop yourself is to be convinced that you don't want to do them (which is different from knowing that you ought not to do them).

Friends, painkillers, prayer and rewarding yourself for small successes will all help. However, a change of attitude is the most important element of a change of behaviour. To know that you will be a more attractive person without the habit is a formidable encouragement. See it as part of the process of becoming more fully human, and feeling increasingly like the delightful person God has always seen when he looks at you.

H o w   m u c h ?

This need not cost anything if you have sufficient willpower, but the alternative behaviour needs to be something that you feel is a small treat, so it may have a financial implication.

At least thirty days are required free from an automatic behaviour before you can be confident that you will master it.

You are most likely to think

I am a strong person, and I shall now use that strength in a good way.

You are least likely to think

That was a doddle!

Don't!

Don't beat yourself up if you lapse – that's just another bad habit. Instead, have a quiet conversation with yourself and start the process again.

To help you reflect

I have the desire to do what is good, but I cannot carry it out. For what I do is not the good I want to do; no, the evil I do not want to do – this I keep on doing . . . What a wretched man I am! Who will rescue me from this body of death? Thanks be to God – through Jesus Christ our Lord!
Romans 7.18, 19, 25

You were called to be free. But do not use your freedom to indulge the sinful nature; rather, serve one another in love.
Galatians 5.13

Who says?

Be both a servant and free: a servant in that you are subject to God, but free in that you are not enslaved to anything – either to empty praise or to any of the passions.
John of Apamea, monk, about 400–450

	The date I broke a bad habit

	The behaviour I changed

The process I went through to break this behaviour	

	What I will remember between here and heaven

15 Learn New Testament Greek

H O W ? For those who study theology at a university or in preparation for ordination, training to read the New Testament in its original language will almost certainly form part of the course. Universities the length and breadth of the country offer this (Belfast, Aberdeen, Durham, Kent, Bangor and so on), and so do Bible colleges (a full list can be found at www.ukbiblecolleges.com).

For those who cannot study in this way, there are still opportunities to make a start, which will in itself offer insights into the Bible and its translations. Investigate short courses of part-time study. For instance, there has recently been a one-term course of weekly lessons at Cardiff University, a residential weekend at Ushaw College (County Durham), and a summer school at St John's College, Nottingham. It is also possible to make New Testament Greek one of the modules in a distance learning course such as the Certificate in Christian Studies from St John's, Nottingham.

A taste of learning the language can be found at www.ntgreek.net, where a great deal of self-discipline could allow you to cover the equivalent of the first year of a Bible college course at no expense.

HOW EXTREME?

Here → ① ② ③ ④ ❺ → Heaven

What should I expect?

The New Testament was written in Greek, and every translation into another language adds and loses something. For example, Jesus' claim to be 'the bread of life' was full of meaning for his original followers. But bread is not the staple food in every country of the world. Japanese Christians know bread as the food that only foreigners eat. So in Japan, interpreters of the Bible have a choice between translating Jesus' words as, 'I am the bread of life', which is accurate but misleading, or, 'I am the rice of life', which conveys exactly what Jesus meant, but not what he said.

This is an extreme example of ten thousand choices that translators make in order to bring us the Bible in a form we can comprehend. Some are minor (should prices be given in ancient denarii or modern pounds?) and others major (did Jesus offer to save lives or to save souls, because the word he used can mean either?). Understanding the language is the way through which you can get closest to knowing the original intention of the writers of the Gospels and letters. It brings one eye-opening discovery after another.

How much?

 The ten week course at Cardiff University cost £58. The weekend course at Ushaw College cost £130. The summer school at St John's College was £225. These prices are typical of similar programmes in other locations.

 Although a short course will give you the skills and enthusiasm to go further, it will probably take a year's regular study in order to read with confidence.

![icon] **Who says?**

One of the many divine qualities of the Bible is this – that it does not yield its secrets to the irreverent and the censorious.
James Packer, theologian

 You are most likely to think

The language of the Gospels is more rich with meaning than I ever realized.

 You are least likely to think

Verily I say unto thee, only that which the King James Version saith is the Word of God.

Don't!

Don't accidentally sign up for a course in classical Greek, which is a different language.

To help you reflect

Our dear brother Paul [writes] with the wisdom that God gave him. He writes the same way in all his letters . . . His letters contain some things that are hard to understand, which ignorant and unstable people distort, as they do the other Scriptures, to their own destruction. Therefore, dear friends, since you already know this, be on your guard.
2 Peter 3.15–17

[Paul wrote:] We do not write you anything you cannot read or understand. And I hope that, as you have understood us in part, you will come to understand fully, that you can boast of us just as we will boast of you in the day of the Lord Jesus.
2 Corinthians 1.13, 14

The date I started to learn New Testament Greek

The course I am following

The first words I learnt, and their meanings

 What I will remember between here and heaven

---

16 Milk a cow

HOW? First, the easy part: explaining how to milk a cow by hand. Put a stool next to the cow's udder and sit with your head resting on its flank. Clean the udder. Place a metal bucket under the teats. Take one teat in the palm of your hand. Squeeze it at the top with your thumb and forefinger, then progressively close the rest of your fingers around the teat, forcing the milk out in a stream. Release your grip and repeat it. When you are confident, use the other hand too, and develop a rhythm until the udder softens and the flow of milk declines.

Cows produce 30 litres of milk every day – enough to fill 100 glasses. They like routine, so it takes time for them to get used to a new person touching them. It may be better for an experienced person to start, before you take over. Try not to pull the teat or do anything else that will hurt the cow – it won't forget!

Next, the difficult part: finding a place where it is possible to learn the skill. Dairy farms are mechanized, and have large numbers of cattle. Milking a cow by hand will involve making a good relationship with a farmer who does not produce milk as a commercial venture, but has a small number of cows. It is sometimes possible to milk a cow on a farm that opens as a tourist attraction, such as Boydells Farm, Essex, Shortwood Family Farm, Herefordshire, or Park Hall, Shropshire. This, although enjoyable, is not an authentic experience.

HOW EXTREME?

Here → ① ② ③ ❹ ⑤ → Heaven

What should I expect?

Milk comes to us homogenized and pasteurized in a carton designed to pour easily. There is almost no tactile relationship with the natural world in the way we feed ourselves, so anything you can do to be more aware of the way you are connected to other living creatures is likely to enhance your appreciation of life.

The milk in the bucket under a cow has hair and hay (and worse) floating in it, which needs to be strained. It is a reminder that the world God has placed us in, although spectacular in its provision of good food, is full of mess and muddle. Giving humans the responsibility to farm and care for it is his way of crafting an orderly environment in which every part of the creation is dependent on every other part in a delicate ecological balance. Divorcing yourself from that process makes it easier to damage the balance, and we do that at our peril.

How much?

If you are the personal guest of a farmer this may not cost anything. Farms with visitor centres have admission charges of between £4 and £7, with reductions for children.

A machine milks a cow in five to eight minutes. Experienced milkmaids of past centuries took about as long to milk a cow by hand, but could only deal with one animal at a time. Frankly, if you are new to it and so is the cow, it might take an hour.

Who says?

The cow is of the bovine ilk;
One end is moo, the other, milk.
Ogden Nash, poet, 1902–1971

You are most likely to think

Now that the food I eat, packaged and processed, looks so little like the living organism from which it came, I must force myself to remember how dependent I am on those who farm God's land.

You are least likely to think

Isn't farming romantic!

Don't!

Don't forget that even nice cows kick!

To help you reflect

[The Lord will] send you rain for the seed you sow in the ground, and the food that comes from the land will be rich and plentiful. In that day your cattle will graze in broad meadows.
Isaiah 30.23

Godliness with contentment is great gain. For we brought nothing into the world, and we can take nothing out of it. But if we have food and clothing, we will be content with that.
1 Timothy 6.6–8

	The date I milked a cow
	Where and what breed?
	How much milk was produced?
	What I will remember between here and heaven

17 Light a candle

HOW? Put the candle in front of you in a safe setting. Light it. Begin by watching the flame and taking in its motion. Remind yourself that God the Holy Spirit is symbolized by flame, and be conscious that the Spirit is present with you. After a while begin to tell God of your fears, hopes and joys. As the flame moves, be aware that God is alive and allow that truth to have an impact on the concerns that are in your mind.

HOW EXTREME?

Here → **①** ② ③ ④ ⑤ → Heaven

What should I expect?

Increasingly, lighted candles are used to bring people of all religions and none together in moments of shared spirituality. They can be used to emphasize aspirations such as the release of hostages, justice for those who suffer, or public sorrow after a tragedy. It may be that you light a candle under those circumstances.

But equally, you may do this as a private act of devotion, since lighting a candle and then extinguishing it can mark the beginning and end of a personal prayer to God. It helps concentration to know that a specific period of time, while the flame burns, is marked out as special.

Lighting candles or lamps is a very ancient religious tradition, so be conscious of centuries of humans using light to bring them close to God. The Jews in the tabernacle, and then the Temple, made use of lamps, so it was not surprising that Christians in the years immediately after Jesus did the same, carrying lights into their evening service. The leaders of the church wrote about their importance not just to illuminate the room, but also to acknowledge their need for God to guide them, like a torch on a dark night, and to give them joy.

In Christian worship, candles have been used specifically to recognize that Jesus called himself 'the Light of the World'. For that reason candles have often been lit at moments when Jesus is recognized uniquely as the Lord, such as baptisms or on Easter Sunday. Candles are also used by Christians to draw special attention to moments that require concentrated attention or honour, so many churches light candles at the start of an act of worship, or make them prominent when the New Testament is read. Some also put them in places where their light reminds everyone of the importance of particular people and activities, such as in front of images of Jesus or saints, or the bread and wine of communion.

A tea-light costs a few pence. Substantial and decorative candles cost £5 or even more.

The longer you spend doing this, the more detail you will notice in the pattern of the flame, and the more your attention will focus on goodness, hope and trust. Start with three or four minutes, and let the time increase as the habit grows.

 Who says?

How far that little candle throws his beams. So shines a good deed in a naughty world.
Portia, in The Merchant of Venice, *William Shakespeare, 1564–1616*

You are most likely to think

The entry of light will always change a dark place. But it is impossible for darkness ever to enter a place and extinguish the light. Knowing this makes it easier to believe that goodness will never be overcome by evil. Hope is imperishable.

 You are least likely to think

This place could do with some more noise and bustle.

Don't!

Don't leave a candle burning unattended.

To help you reflect

You, O Lord, keep my lamp burning;
my God turns my darkness into light.
With your help I can advance against a troop;
with my God I can scale a wall.
As for God, his way is perfect;
the word of the Lord is flawless.
He is a shield for all who take refuge in him.
Psalm 18.28–30

The light shines on in the dark, and the darkness has never mastered it.
John 1.5 (New English Bible)

The date I lit a candle as an act of devotion to God

The colour and shape of the candle

The people and places in my mind as I reflected

What I will remember between here and heaven

18 Go on a retreat

HOW? A retreat is a planned time of spiritual refreshment in a beautiful setting. Because retreats are unhurried, they offer you a chance to reflect on the people and events that are significant in your life, to put them in the context of your experience of God, and to look ahead to the future. Usually a retreat involves sustained times of silence, which is the way many people are able to see past the surface of events and seek their meaning.

However, most retreats offer activity as well, in order to stimulate thoughts to dwell on in the silence. There may be a daily talk, or one-to-one meetings with someone who can guide you through the retreat and suggest what you might read or think about. On themed retreats you can be part of a group involved in a creative activity – for instance, painting, walking or dance – bringing that experience into your prayer.

At www.retreats.org.uk there are links to retreat centres in the UK, all of which list their programmes for the coming year. Their journal *Retreats* is available annually to give more details and can be purchased online. Some centres organize drop-in days so that you can have a taste of what a longer retreat would involve.

HOW EXTREME?

Here → ① ② **❸** ④ ⑤ → Heaven

What should I expect?

Most lives are filled with noise. Most waking hours are spent surrounded by people. Most days are dictated by the clock. A retreat allows you to see what happens if all three constraints are taken away. Many people find that what happens is that they experience the presence of God in a revitalizing way.

This is not escapism, which would simply lead to you returning unchanged to the usual pressures. You bring the pressures and problems with you, but often discover that in a new and inspiring setting, previously unexplored ways of thinking about them open up. The circumstances that transform them can be as simple as a good night's sleep. But you will also be able to talk to someone wise, to pray in a different setting, and to know that no one requires you to meet a target or achieve a result. In circumstances in which you need to make a decision, or find courage and direction, a retreat is the setting in which God can allow those things to take place gently.

Don't!

Don't go with the expectation that others there will chat to you. If what you really seek is company, choose a group holiday rather than a retreat.

How much?

Prices vary, but the typical cost is £40 for every day you spend in residence. Some retreat houses with simpler facilities and programmes charge considerably less.

For a silent retreat, two days and nights is usually long enough to quieten yourself fully. Organized programmes more typically run for five days.

Who says?

If the world knew how happy we are it would, out of sheer envy, invade our retreats, and the times of the Desert Fathers would return, when the solitudes were more populous than the cities.
Madeleine Sophie Barat, French nun, 1779–1865

You are most likely to think

I am going to carry this refreshment with me back into my daily life, and God will give me the energy to do what is right and good.

You are least likely to think

I'm only fulfilled when I'm busy.

To help you reflect

Because so many people were coming and going that they did not even have a chance to eat, [Jesus] said to [his disciples], 'Come with me by yourselves to a quiet place and get some rest.' So they went away by themselves in a boat to a solitary place.
Mark 6.31–32

Oh, that I had the wings of a dove!
I would fly away and be at rest –
I would flee far away and stay in the desert;
I would hurry to my place of shelter,
far from the tempest and storm . . .
But I call to God, and the Lord saves me.
Evening, morning and noon I cry out in distress,
and he hears my voice.
Psalm 55.6–8, 16, 17

The date I went on a retreat

Where?

My most significant thoughts

What I will remember between here and heaven

19 Make a will

HOW? Making a will usually involves a solicitor. If your intentions for what should happen to your possessions after you die are simple (for instance, if you do not own property or intend to leave everything to one family member) you may be able to use a form on the internet or a pack from a bookshop, and draw up the will yourself. However, be aware that a badly made will can be costly and distressing to put right after your death.

It is preferable to visit a solicitor, having thought in advance about what you want to happen to the things you own. Find a local solicitor from the telephone directory or by entering your postcode in the search facility of www.lawsociety.org.uk (where there are also links to the Law Societies of Scotland and Ireland).

If you die without making a will, there are legal rules that determine what happens, but it is quite possible that it will not be what you hoped or assumed would take place.

HOW EXTREME?

Here → ① ❷ ③ ④ ⑤ → Heaven

What should I expect?

Make a list of your property, savings, and objects that are important because they are valuable or loved. Decide to whom you would like to give all these things (they can be divided however you choose), and whether you would like to donate some to a charity. If you are a parent to children under 18, think about who will look after them. Decide on two people on whom you can rely to make sure these instructions are carried out (executors). Then ask two others to come and witness you signing the document (one can be the solicitor, but neither should be people who will gain from your will).

The experience of making a will is both selfish and selfless – selfish because you can decide precisely what you want and no one (except in rare circumstances) can argue; selfless because it saves the people you love trauma and uncertainty at a time when they will be grieving that you are not present.

Although it deals with your death, you will not find yourself thinking morbidly. Instead you will be focusing on the people and things that bring you most happiness in life. It is a pleasure for most people to do this, knowing that its impact will be gratitude and joy. Treat it as an act of thanksgiving to God for all you enjoy about being alive.

How much?

A do-it-yourself pack costs about £20. If a solicitor is involved, he or she will tell you the price before work begins – expect between £100 and £200. Will Aid is a scheme under which solicitors prepare your will free of charge in return for a donation of £65 upwards to charity (www.willaid.org.uk).

If you have planned in advance, it should take less than an hour.

Who says?

When it comes time to die, make sure all you have to do is die.
Jim Elliot, martyred missionary to the Auca tribe of Ecuador, 1927–1956

You are most likely to think

As a result of what I have just done, the sadness that is felt after my death will change into rejoicing and improved lives for family, friends, charities, even people whom I have never met.

You are least likely to think

That was depressing.

Don't!

Don't be among the half of all adults in the UK who die without having made a will.

To help you reflect

[Jesus said,] 'Be on guard! Be alert! You do not know when that time will come. It's like a man going away: he leaves his house and puts his servants in charge, each with his assigned task, and tells the one at the door to keep watch.'
Mark 13.32–34

The saying that is written will come true: 'Death has been swallowed up in victory.' Where, O death, is your victory? Where, O death, is your sting?
1 Corinthians 15.54, 55

The date I made my will

Where can my copy of it be found?

Who will rejoice because of what I have done?

What I will remember between here and heaven

20 Visit an Orthodox service

HOW? Visit www.orthodoxengland.org.uk, where you will find a directory of the Orthodox churches in England, Ireland, Scotland and Wales at which services are held regularly in English. Most give times of services. Telephone the number given before you leave home to check the language of the liturgy.

HOW EXTREME?

Here → ① ❷ ③ ④ ⑤ → Heaven

What should I expect?

Before the service, worshippers walk slowly between icons, gazing at them intently, lighting candles in front of or perhaps kissing them. They find a place to stand silently, praying or reading a Bible. The liturgy is almost entirely sung or chanted, with the priest declaring the glory of God and a choir responding in magnificent harmony. The room is charged with spiritual expectation and there is a repeated chant, 'Again and again let us pray in peace to the Lord.' The majority of the service quotes directly from the Bible. Psalms and the Lord's Prayer are sung, litanies chanted, and passages of the Bible read clearly. In rich, extended praise Jesus (and to a lesser extent, Mary, the Bible, and other saints represented by the icons) are honoured.

For most of the service, the priest is partially hidden behind a tall icon screen (*iconostasis*), glimpsed through an open door amid swirling clouds of incense. This is where bread and wine are consecrated in a setting of veneration and mystery. Later they are brought into the body of the church and reverently placed inside the mouth of each communicant (including baptized children) with a spoon. More bread is distributed at the side of the church. Prayers for the world, and for those who are sick, follow. And finally, the priest removes his vestments and preaches a sermon.

Orthodox spirituality has a deep loyalty to the ancient past, and teachings laid down three hundred years after Jesus still have authority. Orthodox Christians consider themselves to have preserved the beliefs of the very first Christians, and that all other churches have broken away from them (notably the Roman Catholic Church, which split from Orthodoxy about a thousand years ago). Orthodox Christians stress that God is unknowable, and that a living relationship with him will reveal more and more, but never all. Prayer and love are the marks of a true Christian, and so all the theological knowledge in history is useless unless it leads into adoration of God and loving service to the world. And it is in liturgical worship, which brings the salvation of the world through Jesus to life all over again, that God and human beings meet.

How much?

Travel expenses, plus offerings to church funds, the poor, and purchase of candles.

A service lasts well over two hours.

You are most likely to think

I have had a glimpse of the rich and glorious mystery of God's plan for all humankind.

You are least likely to think

Jesus is my chum.

Don't!

Don't ask whether someone can sit beside you to explain what is going on – there are no seats! (This rule is waived if you are elderly or unwell.) And don't cause offence by taking communion unless you are a full member of the Orthodox Church.

To help you reflect

So then, brothers and sisters, stand firm and hold to the teachings we passed on to you, whether by word of mouth or by letter. May our Lord Jesus Christ himself and God our Father, who loved us and by his grace gave us eternal encouragement and good hope, encourage your hearts and strengthen you in every good deed and word.
2 Thessalonians 2.15–17

Ascribe to the Lord, O mighty ones,
ascribe to the Lord glory and strength.
Ascribe to the Lord the glory due his name;
worship the Lord in the splendour of his holiness.
Psalm 29.1–2

Who says?

We should always approach God knowing that we do not know him. We must approach the unsearchable, mysterious God who reveals himself as he chooses; whenever we come to him, we are before a God we do not yet know.
Metropolitan Anthony of Sourozh, head of the Orthodox Church in the UK, 1914–2003

	The date I visited an Orthodox service

	Where was the church?

	Adjectives that describe the experience

	What I will remember between here and heaven

21 Watch a birth

HOW? To watch a human birth you must be medically qualified, or the person nominated by a mother-to-be as her 'birth partner'. This can be the father of the baby, or a close friend or relative, or both. Birth partners give vital support and encouragement. There are practical things you can offer too, such as back massage, fetching cool drinks, or being the uncomplaining target of curses!

There are many ways of watching the birth of an animal. For those who live in farming communities or breed dogs it is part of a way of life. Those who live in towns need to make a special effort, and that may involve contacting friends of friends until you reach a hospitable farmer. There are farms open to the public that make a feature of allowing visitors to witness lambs being born in Spring. Wimpole Home Farm, Cambridgeshire, and Newark Farm, Dumfries, encourage visitors during the lambing season (although obviously they cannot guarantee when a birth will take place). At Steamvale Open Farm, Belfast, it is possible to see calves born. The Acorn Venture Urban Farm, Merseyside, and Deen City Farm, South London, both have incubator rooms, and are able to loan an incubator and eggs, usually to a school, so that you can watch chicks hatch.

HOW EXTREME?

Here → ① ② ③ ❹ ⑤ → Heaven

What should I expect?

Watching a birth is an extremely emotional experience (even, in its own way, watching an animal being born). In all cultures, the fact that something begins as intangible love and ends as flesh and bone is a wonder that inspires awe and joy. Our increased understanding of the science that explains it has not diminished our desire to cry out in thanks to God for something that seems miraculous. So expect to have such a strong sense of involvement that your own body strains in sympathy with the mother, and then to feel exhilarated when the new life has entered the world.

Use the experience as a chance to think about your own place in the world. Ask God why, of all the billions of lives that potentially could have begun, it was yours that he chose. Enjoy the fact that you are breathing the air of God's world for a purpose, even if it is hard to ascertain. And then offer the new life that has begun, whether it is human, cat or caterpillar, into the care of the one who has sustained life on this planet for a good reason for so many centuries.

Under the UK National Health Service there is no charge for health care associated with the birth of a child. Farms that open to the public charge between £4 and £7 for adults, with concessionary rates. The cost of borrowing an incubator varies between £65 and £135.

The average length of labour for a first child is 13 hours, and seven for subsequent babies. An elephant is in labour for two whole days, and a rabbit for ten minutes.

Who says?

The passion shown in the birth of a child gives us a glimpse into the passion of God giving birth to creation.
Choan-Seng Song, Taiwanese theologian

You are most likely to think

Birth is a miracle. Life is a miracle. I am a miracle.

You are least likely to think

Life has no meaning.

Don't!

Don't assume that children will be fascinated by animals giving birth – they may find it more repulsive than wondrous.

To help you reflect

You created my inmost being;
you knit me together in my mother's womb.
I praise you because I am fearfully and
*   wonderfully made;*
your works are wonderful, I know that full well.
Psalm 139.13–14

[Jesus said,] 'A woman giving birth to a child has pain because her time has come; but when her baby is born she forgets the anguish because of her joy that a child is born into the world. So with you: now is your time of grief, but I will see you again and you will rejoice, and no one will take away your joy.'
John 16.21, 22

The date I watched a birth

Human or animal?

What circumstances led to me being there?

What I will remember between here and heaven

43

22 Conquer your fear

HOW? Everyone is moderately afraid of something (going to the dentist, for instance – odontophobia). Most people struggle through their aversions because they have them in proportion (you can shrug off the anxious moment when an aeroplane takes off – aviophobia – because the chances of dying in a plane crash are one in 1.5 million). However, for a few people the fear is so intense that it makes life miserable. A fear of eating in public (phagophobia) or of contact with dirt (mysophobia) can so limit what you are able to do that the joy goes out of life.

Start your journey into freedom with a visit to your GP. He or she will recommend treatment, such as Triumph Over Phobia UK, which runs a network of groups in which you can learn to face up to fears in a controlled way, so that the anxiety decreases (www.triumphoverphobia.com). No Panic runs a telephone helpline (0808 8080 545) for anyone who is affected by panic attacks or anxiety disorders. It can provide support, literature or pen-pals for them and their families.

One-to-one behaviour therapy is also available privately, and airlines offer one-day courses that effectively address the fear of flying.

HOW EXTREME?

Here → ① ② ③ ❹ ⑤ → Heaven

What should I expect?

Beneath varied fears lie the same roots – anxieties about failure, rejection or disapproval. There are two steps to dealing with them. The first is to build up your inner strength so that you are better able to cope. The second is to identify and understand your fears, because knowing how and why they are damaging you removes the power they have.

Treatments usually begin by learning techniques that induce calm, such as breathing exercises. Then the process involves being exposed to the things that frighten you in a gradual, structured way. It begins with a gentle encounter with whatever causes your fear in a way in which, with the support of others, you feel quite safe. It then builds in intensity to a point at which you are able to face difficult situations without panic. This is accompanied by conversation, analysis and (if you are conquering your fear in the company of Christians) prayer.

Don't!

Don't overlook the fact that God has given us the ability to fear for a good reason. Fear of standing on precarious cliff-tops (acrophobia) or walking alone down dark alleys (achluophobia) is entirely sensible.

How much?

Neither Triumph Over Phobia UK nor No Panic make a charge. The prices charged by behaviour therapists vary enormously from £20 to £70 per session. A Virgin Atlantic 'Flying without fear' course costs £234.

Not as long as you might imagine. Although it will not obliterate fear altogether, five or six hours of treatment will make a genuine difference to your levels of anxiety.

You are most likely to think

'Free at last! Free at last! Thank God Almighty, I am free at last.'

You are least likely to think

I'm planning to develop ecclesiophobia. (It's a fear of going to church.)

To help you reflect

God has said, 'Never will I leave you; never will I forsake you.' So we say with confidence, 'The Lord is my helper; I will not be afraid. What can human beings do to me?'
Hebrews 13.5, 6

My son, preserve sound judgement and discernment, do not let them out of your sight; they will be life for you, an ornament to grace your neck. Then you will go on your way in safety, and your foot will not stumble; when you lie down, you will not be afraid; when you lie down, your sleep will be sweet. Have no fear of sudden disaster or of the ruin that overtakes the wicked, for the Lord will be your confidence.
Proverbs 3.21–26

Who says?

Whenever I hear about Christ as Saviour it appears that he saves from sin – and I don't wish to deny that – but in my experience he does more than that: he releases us from fear, and I think fear is the great killer.
Ivor Smith-Cameron, Indian clergyman

The date I began to tackle my fear

The name of my fear and the length of time it has trapped me

Describe the treatment

What I will remember between here and heaven

23 Grapple with Revelation

HOW? Revelation is the last book in the Bible. It is difficult to read because it is full of symbolism to which we no longer possess the key. Literature like this is called apocalyptic (Daniel 7—12 and Matthew 24 are other examples). Its characteristic is a vision that God triumphs at the end of a devastating battle against the forces of evil, pictured as fantastical beasts. Its original readers recognized this kind of writing, so the author did not bother to explain it.

Guides include the slim and readable *How to Read the Book of Revelation* by Ian Paul (Grove) or the weighty and exhaustive *Revelation* by Ben Witherington (New Cambridge Bible Commentary). Care should be taken using the internet to research Revelation, because its mystical content entices many who see in it allusions to events taking place in the world today. A guide that is worth taking seriously comes from a theologian who tells you even-handedly about different ways of interpreting the book, not someone who ingeniously connects 'hidden meanings' to produce a crackpot theory that the world will end at midnight.

HOW EXTREME?

Here → ① **❷** ③ ④ ⑤ → Heaven

What should I expect?

You will discover four major ways of interpreting Revelation. The 'preterist' view understands that every event described by the writer alludes to something that was actually happening in his own day (for example, the evil Babylon refers to Rome, where Christians were being persecuted in the first century). The 'futurist' view sees the book predicting the way the world will end (a view that was popular in the 20th century, with many books encouraging Christians that faith will take them away from tribulation and straight to heaven when Jesus returns). The 'historicist' view is that the mysterious events symbolize the whole sweep of history from the 1st century to the future end of the world (Protestants of the 16th century popularized this view, using it to attack Roman Catholicism, but they were wrong to presume that they were the last generation who would inhabit this planet, and there is no reason why those who think it today are any wiser). An 'idealist' interpretation is that the writer did not set out to prophesy events, but to inspire Christians to persevere through suffering to the triumphant end.

Don't!

Don't take any sentence of Revelation literally, because that was never the writer's intention.

Ian Paul's booklet costs £2.95. Ben Witherington's commentary costs £15.99. A Bible costs between £7 and £15, but you can read Revelation free online at www.biblegateway.com.

It takes 90 minutes to read Revelation. However, looking up theologians' comments will take several evenings.

Who says?

The book of Revelation [assures] its readers that this world belongs to God and not to the forces of evil. Through the use of vivid and powerful imagery it emphasizes that God will act to put things right, no matter how long such action may seem to be delayed . . . a new world, where sin, misery and evil have no further place.
John Drane, theologian

You are most likely to think

I hardly understood a word, but it's clear that, because of Jesus, the world is in safe hands and I'm on the winning side.

You are least likely to think

The Norman conquest, the great fire of London, the moon landings, the gridlock on the M25 – they are all predicted here.

To help you reflect

These words are trustworthy and true . . . Blessed is he who keeps the words of the prophecy in this book . . . Worship God!' Then [the angel] told me, 'Do not seal up the words of the prophecy of this book, because the time is near.' . . . He who testifies to these things says, 'Yes, I am coming soon.' Amen. Come, Lord Jesus!
Revelation 22.6, 7, 9, 10, 20

Command certain persons not to teach false doctrines any longer nor to devote themselves to myths and endless genealogies. These promote controversies rather than God's work – which is by faith. The goal of this command is love, which comes from a pure heart, a good conscience and a sincere faith.
1 Timothy 1.3–5

The date I studied Revelation

The most important things I discovered

My hopes and fears for human destiny

What I will remember between here and heaven

24 Be still

HOW? This may not be as obvious as it seems. Seek out a time and place where you can be reasonably certain that you will not be disturbed. It will be virtually impossible to find complete silence, but at least try to exclude the noise of music, broadcasting or chatter.

Set an alarm to go off at the end of time you have allocated. Seat yourself comfortably. Shut your eyes. See the shapes and colours in the darkness behind your eyelids. Slowly become conscious of your breathing. Use this to help you get in touch with your body, and to disclose the level of tension within it. Tense all your muscles, and then relax them one at a time, starting with your toes and progressing to your head, until there is no tension left. Inhale deeply, slowly tilting your head back. Then exhale, allowing your head slowly to rock forward. Do this several times.

Become silent, first outwardly and then inwardly. Pay attention to the fact that God is present. Don't reflect on any particular thing, but let thoughts take you by surprise. Don't ask God for anything. Create a space that he can fill with his love for you.

HOW EXTREME?

Here → **❶** ② ③ ④ ⑤ → Heaven

What should I expect?

The first thing you will be aware of is the sound of your breathing. Thank God for something you never usually hear. You may be still enough to hear other unexpected sounds, such as bird song or distant traffic. They may help the process, rather than distracting you, so thank God for another thing you do not often listen to.

Use each breath as a means of centring your thoughts on God. As you exhale, tell God that you are pushing away your anxiety over your job. As you inhale, tell God that you are breathing in his peace. As you exhale, tell God that you are pushing away your frustration about your church. As you inhale, tell God that you are breathing in his faithfulness. If it is possible, let God progressively occupy all your attention. If your mind wanders to something concerning your home or family, make that one of the things you consciously breathe out, and draw in a breath that is full of things you appreciate about God. Then listen once again.

Make the most of the fact that for this period of time, no one has any expectations of you. You and God can simply be at one with each other – lovingly, grumpily or tiredly. At the end, thank him for having been with you.

Don't!

Don't go into the exercise with any specific expectations. If ideas or feelings come, fine. If not, it is also fine. Simply enjoy the absence of noise and activity.

 Nothing.

 Ten minutes, or perhaps more.

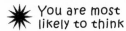 You are most likely to think

How is it that ten minutes of boredom feel like ten hours, but ten minutes of silence feel like ten seconds?

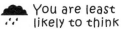 You are least likely to think

Where are the Rolling Stones when you need them?

 Who says?

Silence is precious: but we have to pay the price it demands. Silence does not reveal its treasures until we are willing to wait in darkness and emptiness.
Olive Wyon, devotional writer, 1890–1976

To help you reflect

Because of the Lord's great love we are not consumed,
for his compassions never fail.
They are new every morning; great is your faithfulness.
I say to myself, 'The Lord is my portion; therefore I will wait for him.'
The Lord is good to those whose hope is in him,
to the one who seeks him;
it is good to wait quietly for the salvation of the Lord.
It is good for a man to bear the yoke while he is young.
Let him sit alone in silence, for the Lord has laid it on him.
Lamentations 3.22–28

Be still, and know that I am God;
I will be exalted among the nations,
I will be exalted in the earth.
Psalm 46.10

The date I sought stillness

Where?

Adjectives that describe the experience

What I will remember between here and heaven

25 Grow something you eat

HOW? Make a plan for growing something that fits the circumstances in which you live. If you live in a flat, germinate sprouts, such as alfalfa or mung beans. It is possible to buy trays for sprouting beans, but any glass bowl can be used, covered, but with holes allowing air in. Soak the seeds overnight in water and drain them. Spread them, remembering that they will increase in size many times over. Keep them in the dark for the first three days, then bring them into the light, adding a small amount of water twice a day. They should be ready to eat, as part of a salad, in seven days.

With even less space, grow cress or mustard, which require only a plate and some kitchen paper. Sprinkle the seeds, add water, and put the plate in a place that is reasonably warm and light. After five days, add this to egg or cheese sandwiches.

If you have a little space outside, grow herbs in a container at least 25cm wide and deep. Any pot will do, as long as it has holes in the bottom so that it drains (a growbag has a mixture of soil and compost already prepared for you). Try growing parsley, because it can be added to almost anything you cook. In Spring, put compost in the container and push the parsley seeds in 2cm deep. Pour boiling water over them, and put the pot where it will get a few hours of sunshine every day. Water the seeds on days when it doesn't rain and hope for the best. Four weeks later you should have parsley to cut.

Garlic also grows effortlessly if you pull apart a bulb in October, plant individual cloves 2cm deep and 10cm apart, and pull them up in June.

HOW EXTREME?

Here → ① ❷ ③ ④ ⑤ → Heaven

What should I expect?

There are five good reasons for growing something to eat. First and most obvious, fruit and vegetables are good for you. Second, the taste and crispness of such fresh produce greatly exceeds anything you buy in a supermarket. Third, you will know exactly what chemicals have and haven't been added. Fourth, you know that transporting it from where it grew to your plate added nothing to global warming. And finally, you will be part of the day-to-day miracle through which God constantly enriches the planet with life and growth.

Don't!

Don't abandon what you have planted. Water it little and often.

💰 A tray for sprouting costs about £7, and the mung or alfalfa beans to grow in it cost about £2 for a large packet. Parsley, cress or other herb seeds cost £1 for a packet. A growbag costs about £8.

🕐 All these minimum-effort foods require 20 minutes to begin with, and subsequently a few seconds daily.

You are most likely to think

Our God, who created everything out of nothing, goes on and on making life begin even in the most unpromising circumstances.

☁ You are least likely to think

The best way to eat is as individuals each sitting in front of our own television.

Who says?

There is something about the simple tasks of washing, peeling and cooking a carrot, picking herbs and adding them to the pot, growing a spindly tomato plant and eating its fruit, that makes it transparent that in our living we are ordered to a Creator. If we eat at all, and if there is work for our hands to do, it is because [God has provided] it for us.

Clare Watkins, theologian

To help you reflect

I know that there is nothing better for people than to be happy and do good while they live. That each of them may eat and drink, and find satisfaction in all their toil – this is the gift of God.
Ecclesiastes 3.12, 13

'I will bring back my exiled people Israel,' [declares the Lord].
'They will rebuild the ruined cities and live in them.
They will plant vineyards and drink their wine;
they will make gardens and eat their fruit.'
Amos 9.14

The date I first ate something I had grown

What was it?

The people with whom I ate the meal

What I will remember between here and heaven

26 Blog

HOW? A blog (or weblog, to use its full name) is a personal diary made public on the internet. Websites such as www.blogger.com provide a structure that allows you to do so simply. As you update it regularly, visitors to your blog can comment on what you have written or email you. You can decide whether you want everyone in the world to be able to read your thoughts, or whether to protect them with a password that you make known only to your friends.

You can use the space as a daily pulpit, a political commentary, a journal of your experiences during an interesting phase of your life, a photo album, a record of what God is teaching you, or a collaborative space in which to discuss ideas. You create a profile that describes the content of your blog so that people who share your interests become aware that you are writing.

When you first visit the website that facilitates this, you will be asked to create an account by supplying your name and email address. You can choose a colour, name and layout so that your blog looks distinctive. Then you are ready to post your first entry. Send the URL (the internet address at which to find your blog) to anyone whom you hope might be interested in reading it, and publicize it by adding it to business cards, emails, Christmas cards, or anywhere that will encourage readers to access it (which will in turn encourage you to keep writing).

HOW EXTREME?

Here → ① ② ❸ ④ ⑤ → Heaven

What should I expect?

The value of blogging is not only that you can communicate with others, but also that you can organize your own thoughts about what is happening to you and to the world. Keep your posts interesting so that reading them is a pleasure, not a chore. (Your trip to the supermarket is not interesting; your decision to avoid going to supermarkets for a month is!)

You will find yourself looking at what you do through other people's eyes. This will make you increasingly aware that what you do and write are witnesses to your Christian beliefs. The number of people visiting your site will be small at the beginning, but it will grow, and so will your opportunity to influence society for good.

How much?

 There is no charge to use www.blogger.com. Sites such as www.livejournal.com offer extra features for about £2 per month.

 Blogging for 15 minutes daily keeps the content fresh and encourages visitors to return more effectively than spending a whole evening monthly.

Don't!

Don't publish anything about the failings or illnesses of friends or family that would be upsetting for them to read in a public forum.

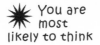

You are most likely to think

The things God is teaching me about being alive are important, and this is a way of sharing them.

You are least likely to think

I am getting blogged down in this!

Who says?

I do hope blogging becomes a tool that Christians embrace and learn to wield effectively. It's a great way to be in the culture and comment on it. It's also a great way to sharpen up your own ability to think about the arguments of others and make your own rhetoric more effective . . . Our blogs should be well-written, interesting and demonstrate a decent level of thought and reasoning power. There are plenty of Christians out there who can and should start up a blog and get in the game.
Martin Roth, Australian commentator and blogger

To help you reflect

We proclaim to you what we have seen and heard, so that you also may have fellowship with us. And our fellowship is with the Father and with his Son, Jesus Christ. We write this to make our joy complete. This is the message we have heard from him and declare to you: God is light; in him there is no darkness at all.
1 John 1.3–5

May the words of my mouth and the meditation of my heart be pleasing in your sight, O Lord, my Rock and my Redeemer.
Psalm 19.14

The date I began my blog

The URL

What I have written about so far

What I will remember between here and heaven

27 Write to a prisoner on Death Row

HOW? The charity Bridge the Gap facilitates a penpal scheme putting people in the UK in touch with prisoners on Death Row in the United States (as well as those in British and American jails not facing execution). An application form to be a penpal can be found at www.btguk.org (click 'Death Row') or from PO Box 783, Croydon, CR9 1BT.

Their advice is to write twice a month to the person whose name and address they supply. Write letters full of hope and friendship. There is no need to ask why your penpal is in jail – if he or she wants to tell you, it will emerge as trust grows. Resist the temptation to preach, but write about your faith in a natural way as you describe the routines of your life. Prisoners are extremely short of money and need to pay for stamps, so it is worth asking whether prison regulations allow you to send some American stamps to make replying easier. However, be aware that desperation (or opportunism) may prompt someone to ask you to send unrealistic amounts of money. You may need to resist this kindly, and also to resist romantic overtures. Using the PO Box address of Bridge the Gap, from which they forward letters to you, allows you to be absolutely sure of your security.

HOW EXTREME?

Here → ① ② ③ ❹ ⑤ → Heaven

What should I expect?

About 3,500 men and 65 women are on Death Row awaiting execution in the USA. The average length of time between sentencing and execution is seven years, but some live on Death Row for more than a decade. Almost all the prisoners are from poor backgrounds. They live in harsh conditions, and many are abandoned by their families, so they have little contact with the outside world. Letters are a lifeline.

Writing to someone on Death Row can be extremely rewarding, but also full of problems. To begin a relationship but then lapse can be distressing for a prisoner. And for death to cut short a friendship that has developed can be devastating for the writer. However, writing to someone in prison is certain to increase your awareness of what it means to be alive, and your appreciation of your own freedom. Jesus included prisoners among six groups of needy people whose treatment was the measure of what it means practically to serve him. The amount of care we can find for those who are utterly despised reveals the amount of care we have for him.

An airmail letter to the USA costs 50 pence.

 30 minutes every fortnight is reasonable, although there are no limits.

 You are most likely to think

Life (every single life) is precious.

 You are least likely to think

The death penalty should be restored.

Don't!

Don't forget, as you write and pray, that whether or not the person you are communicating with is guilty of it, there is a family also in need of compassion, who is grieving the loss of a loved one who has been murdered.

 Who says?

I'm a Christian, but feel lost. Could you write me? Looking for a little sunshine through these dark and cold walls they call prison, and things of interest during these lockdown times . . . I have dreams and hopes, and know how to keep a smile on mine and others' faces. It just comes slow at times in a place like this. So if you get the urge to shed a little light my way, fear not, I do have a lot to say.
Trent Wacker, Pelican Bay State Prison, California

To help you reflect

Remember those in prison as if you were their fellow prisoners, and those who are mistreated as if you yourselves were suffering.
Hebrews 13.3

Help us, O God our Saviour, for the glory of your name;
deliver us and forgive our sins for your name's sake . . .
May the groans of the prisoners come before you;
by the strength of your arm preserve those condemned to die.
Psalm 79.9, 11

	The date I began to write to a prisoner on death row

	His or her name

	Some things I have learnt about him or her

	What I will remember between here and heaven

28 Tell the preacher you disagree

HOW? The word 'sermon' originally meant discourse or conversation, and the sermons of the early Church may have been closer to dialogues in which ideas, Scripture and the experience of having known Jesus came together in order to pursue the truth. Today, a person who disagrees with a sermon is more likely to comment on it behind the preacher's back. Although this appears to keep the peace, it does not advance anyone's thinking.

An alternative is to ask the preacher for an opportunity to discuss how he or she reached particular conclusions, and enquire how the preacher prefers to discuss such things – in person, or by letter, email or telephone.

Prepare carefully for the conversation, being clear in your mind whether the element with which you disagreed was part of the style, the information or the interpretation. Stress what you did appreciate about what the preacher said, and make that the context for explaining what you couldn't agree with. Ask for clarification (because you may, after all, have misunderstood) and develop a conversation rather than hammering home your point. Conclude at a stage at which there is no 'winner', but you both understand why the other thinks as he or she does.

HOW EXTREME?

Here → ① ② ❸ ④ ⑤ → Heaven

What should I expect?

This will not be an easy conversation. Some preachers believe that they have delivered God's message and may find it hard to come to terms with the possibility that they might have been mistaken. Others are lacking in confidence and may crumple as if they have been personally attacked. Expect to have to communicate with gentleness, as well as having to gather your own courage together.

If you come away understanding each other's desire to honour God in your thinking and speaking, you have succeeded, even if you have not come to a common mind. Other positive outcomes include a discussion group so that issues such as this can be opened up, an exchange of suggestions of books that have shaped your thinking, or the chance to pray together for the truth to set people free.

How much?

The price of a stamp or phone call.

This is unlikely to be the most important thing the preacher has to deal with to build the Kingdom of God. Spending more than an hour discussing it would probably not repay the investment.

Don't!

Don't challenge the speaker immediately after he or she has preached (an extremely vulnerable time). Wait a couple of days to make contact. Don't be aggressive, and don't give the impression that the entire church is united behind you in opposition – both of which will make the preacher defensive and unable to engage with the issues that are actually important.

 Who says?

It is the worst trial of a preacher's life that he is ever set up on a pedestal, where he himself is seen in a false perspective, and may easily come to see himself as others see him. Still, he does want encouragement sometimes, poor thing! And an honest, loving friend, who blames as well as praises, can give it.
Herbert Hensley Henson, bishop of Durham, 1863–1947

 You are most likely to think

The truth (even when it is awkward, elusive or bruising) is always worth pursuing.

 You are least likely to think

I love telling people how wrong they are.

To help you reflect

[In Ephesus, Paul] took the disciples with him and had discussions daily in the lecture hall of Tyrannus. This went on for two years, so that all the Jews and Greeks who lived in the province of Asia heard the word of the Lord.
Acts 19.9, 10

Don't have anything to do with foolish and stupid arguments, because you know they produce quarrels. And the Lord's servant must not quarrel; instead, he must be kind to everyone, able to teach, not resentful. Those who oppose him he must gently instruct, in the hope that God will grant them repentance leading them to a knowledge of the truth.
2 Timothy 2.23–25

	The date I told the preacher I disagreed

	This is what I disagreed with

	This was the nature of our discussion

	What I will remember between here and heaven

29 Write a hymn

HOW? If you are an experienced musician, you will already have a sense of how a phrase and melody might emerge alongside each other, even if you have never attempted it. This activity is more challenging if you do not play an instrument, which is a good reason to attempt it. Choose an established melody (perhaps a hymn tune or a folk song) and create new words for it. The psalms of the Bible are inexhaustible sources of inspiration, expressing a range of emotions and questions that men and women have addressed to God in every subsequent century. Try to rephrase a line from a psalm in a way that fits naturally into the rhythm of one of the lines of the tune. If it stays in your mind, extend the theme into a verse, and then several. Follow the rhyming pattern of the song's original words.

Some find that composing alongside others inspires them. The magazine *Worship Live* (Stainer & Bell, www.stainer.co.uk) publishes new hymns and develops a network of people interested in hymnwriting through workshops. Passion For Your Name offers a monthly column of advice to songwriters at www.passionforyourname.com, and at its annual festival there are songwriting seminars.

HOW EXTREME?

Here → ① ❷ ③ ④ ⑤ → Heaven

What should I expect?

Write from your heart, expressing concepts that you genuinely feel. The words might state what God is like, or they might be a personal response to God written in the first person. Praise is central to worship, but there is also an important place for hymns that are prayers for justice, statements of commitment, or pleas for forgiveness. Match the nature of the words to the mood of the chosen music.

Be strict with yourself and avoid anything that is too obvious, rhymes that clunk, or lines that that need to be sung in an unnatural way in order to fit the tune. When you have finished, use the song as your own act of worship to God. The main point of composing is to bring joy to him. Show it to friends who are theologically informed or musically talented and ask for their reaction. If they suggest that the hymn would allow others to worship in an uplifting way, explore the possibility of using it at a church. Be ready to revise it after you hear what it sounds like when many people sing it together.

Don't!

Don't waste time looking for a rhyme for God. Anything you try will cause an unintentional laugh.

How much?

A pencil and a sheet of paper cost almost nothing. The price of the Passion For Your Name conference is £80, plus accommodation expenses. An annual subscription to *Worship Live* costs £9 for three issues.

Longer than you expect. Whatever you write can always be improved over subsequent days and weeks.

Who says?

I believe my King suggests a thought, and whispers me a musical line or two, and then I look up and thank him delightedly, and go on with it. That is how my hymns come.
Frances Ridley Havergal, hymnwriter (of 'Take my life and let it be' among others), 1836–1879

You are most likely to think

Dear Lord and Father of mankind,
Forgive our whining ways,
We criticize and can't abide
All hymns composed since Wesley died,
Revitalize our praise,
Revitalize our praise.

You are least likely to think

All people that on earth do dwell,
Sing my new hymn with cheesy voice,
I am tone deaf and cannot spell,
But it's a one-off, so rejoice!

To help you reflect

Speak to one another with psalms, hymns and spiritual songs. Sing and make music in your heart to the Lord, always giving thanks to God the Father for everything.
Ephesians 5.19, 20

Sing to the Lord a new song;
sing to the Lord, all the earth.
Sing to the Lord, praise his name;
proclaim his salvation day after day.
Declare his glory among the nations,
his marvellous deeds among all peoples.
For great is the Lord and most worthy of praise.
Psalm 96.1–4

The date I wrote a hymn

Its title, and its best line

Has it been sung as an act of worship? If so, where and when?

What I will remember between here and heaven

30 Learn to appreciate wine or beer

HOW? Books and television programmes are no substitute for experiencing the taste of wine or beer in a thoughtful manner. Click on 'New to wine?' at www.wineanorak.co.uk for ways to begin to appreciate wine, and www.tastebeer.com for equivalent information about beer. Bookshop shelves overflow with introductions to wine, and the Campaign for Real Ale (CAMRA) publishes directories that encourage people to seek out quality beer.

HOW EXTREME?

Here → ① **❷** ③ ④ ⑤ → Heaven

What should I expect?

Appreciating wine or beer begins with its appearance. Experience helps you anticipate the intensity of red or white wine by its colour. With beer, it is the clarity, colour and head that indicates its style. Smell is vital, and beginners quickly start enjoying previously unnoticed features – scents that remind them of spices or flowers in a wine; hops or butterscotch in a beer. When you have taken a mouthful, take time (swallowing it straight away bypasses most of your tastebuds). In a wine, the flavour will change in your mouth and remind you of other things you have tasted in the past, especially fruits. In a beer, concentrating on its flavour, feel in your mouth and aftertaste will all add to the pleasure you get. Make a note of what you drank and what you thought to compare on future occasions.

Jesus was both loved and criticized because of his appreciation of food and drink. At Cana he turned water not just into wine, but into fine wine. The amount of pleasure wine and beer give increases the more you know about and concentrate on them. Turn that appreciation into thanks for the infinite variety of pleasures that God has given to humans through the senses.

How much?

A one-day course by the Wine Education Service costs £110, and a series of evening classes £185 (www.wine-education-service.co.uk). Adult education courses are less expensive (£53 at Queen's University, Belfast, for instance). *The Richard and Judy Wine Guide* (introduced by Richard Madeley and Judy Finnegan, HarperCollins) is priced at £16.99. The Beer Academy's tasting course costs £145 (www.beeracademy.co.uk), and CAMRA's *Good Beer Guide* is £13.99. The price of a bottle of wine or a pint of beer is too varied to record, but expense is not necessarily a guide to quality.

One day or a series of evenings are a good beginning, but skills improve over many years. However, your appreciation of beer or wine will improve dramatically simply by slowing the speed at which you drink.

Don't!

Don't get drunk, which displays derision for wine or beer, rather than appreciation.

 You are most likely to think

If the old wine on earth tastes this good, whatever will the new wine of heaven be like?

 You are least likely to think

Pity nobody organizes a *Pepsi* tasting.

 Who says?

I would like to have the men of Heaven in my own house, with vats of good cheer laid out for them. I would like to have the three Marys, for their fame is so great. I would like people from every corner of Heaven. I would like them to be cheerful in their drinking. I would like to have Jesus too here amongst them. I would like a great lake of beer for the King of kings. I would like to be watching Heaven's family, drinking it through all eternity.
Brigid, abbess and matron of Christianity in Ireland, 451–525

To help you reflect

Eat your food with gladness, and drink your wine with a joyful heart, for it is now that God favours what you do.
Ecclesiastes 9.7

Jesus said to the servants, 'Fill the jars with water'; so they filled them to the brim . . . The master of the banquet tasted the water that had been turned into wine. He did not realize where it had come from, though the servants who had drawn the water knew. Then he called the bridegroom aside and said, 'Everyone brings out the choice wine first and then the cheaper wine after the guests have had too much to drink; but you have saved the best till now.'
John 2.7–10

The date I began to appreciate wine or beer

This is what I drank

Something I have learnt about taste

What I will remember between here and heaven

61

31 Keep a Sabbath

HOW? In your diary, look up the next four Sundays (or, if that is unrealistic, another regular day of the week) and write 'special' in the space. Make plans that will allow these to become the most enjoyable and relaxing days of the seven that make up each week.

First, decide what will definitely not happen on those days (for instance, household chores, inadequate sleep, trudging through the supermarket). Organize how and when these will be done instead.

Second, decide what you will do instead. Include things that you will recognize as a treat from God to you, and also things that are, in a sense, a treat from you to God. Follow the biblical principles of a Sabbath by including space for worship, space for reflecting on life, and space for administering care to others.

After four Sabbaths, analyse whether this is improving the rhythm of your life and consider extending it. If habits you have got into make the day arduous (such as obligations to cook a special dinner, or even to sit through a service that stifles your joy in being a Christian) think creatively about alternatives.

HOW EXTREME?

Here → ① ❷ ③ ④ ⑤ → Heaven

What should I expect?

At a low-point of their history the Hebrew people were enslaved – no rest, no day off, no care, just the misery of having one's life used as a commodity to achieve wealth for someone else. After they were freed from oppression, they were commanded never to forget what they had been through, and never to replicate it when they became the employers rather than the enslaved. There was to be a Sabbath, one day in seven and one year in seven, that was different. The people rested, the land rested, the livestock rested.

God has always been concerned that human life should have a healthy rhythm. He offers a Sabbath day, once in every seven, not because he wants us to do something awkward to please him, but as a gift that will improve our lives. It is a gift to individuals for refreshment and to society so that once in a while the pressure relents.

To keep a Sabbath in this generation involves being strong enough to resist the 24/7 nature of the culture. However, nothing about the day should make it burdensome (for instance, sparing yourself the chore of shopping is not meant to prevent you buying an ice cream on a sunny afternoon). Expect to feel invigorated by spending one day completely unlike the way you spend the others.

Nothing (although if you have been in the habit of using every last hour to earn every last penny there may be a financial cost to finding a better way).

 24 glorious, life-enhancing hours per week.

Don't!

Don't shrug this off if shift work or circumstances mean that it is impossible to treat Sunday as a Sabbath. Nominate another day to keep special instead.

 Who says?

Sunday clears away the rust of the whole week.
Joseph Addison, poet, 1672–1719

 You are most likely to think

This has rescued me from the remorseless stream of weekdays that stretch from Boxing Day to Christmas Eve.

 You are least likely to think

I can't wait for the alarm to go off on Monday morning.

To help you reflect

For six years you shall sow your land and gather in its yield; but the seventh year you shall let it rest and lie fallow, so that the poor of your people may eat; and what they leave the wild animals may eat . . . Six days you shall do your work, but on the seventh day you shall rest, so that your ox and your donkey may have relief, and your homeborn slave and the resident alien may be refreshed.
Exodus 23.10–12

There remains, then, a Sabbath-rest for the people of God; for anyone who enters God's rest also rests from his own work, just as God did from his. Let us, therefore, make every effort to enter that rest, so that no one will fall.
Hebrews 4.9–11

The date I began to observe a Sabbath

The things I decided not to do

The things I did instead

What I will remember between here and heaven

32 Label your photographs

HOW? Choose a method of organizing your collection. A chronological scheme is best for photographs you have taken, but if you have inherited an unlabelled collection from decades past it may be easier to group them by people or events. If you discover photographs whose subject or date are unknown, *Uncovering your Ancestry through Family Photographs*, by Maureen Taylor, has advice about using clues in the image to track down dates, locations and (through the help of relatives) names and relationships. The clues include clothing, wedding rings, body language, and even the nature of the stock on which the image is printed.

To ensure that the information is never separated from the images, write directly on the back of the photograph with a 2B pencil (not a ball-point pen that will indent the print, nor ink that contains acid). Record the names, the location, the approximate date, and what is taking place. Avoid using self-adhesive labels or tape, because the acid in them irreversibly damages the photos.

HOW EXTREME?

Here → **❶** ② ③ ④ ⑤ → Heaven

What should I expect?

The people of God during the centuries recorded in the Old Testament had a burning desire that they should not be forgotten by future generations. They passed on family stories to their children, and instructed them to do the same. And they left physical reminders, like standing stones beside a river, so that the memory of important moments would be indelible.

Photography has made passing on such stories so easy that we take it for granted, but labelling photographs means that the landmarks of your family history can be recorded before it is too late. As you do it, take the opportunity to sit down with your immediate family and explore the photographs. Laugh and cry over the story of how God led you to where you are now, and the people who shared the route. As well as celebrating happy moments, be honest about times when it went wrong, and how God picked you up and pushed you, battered and protesting, or maybe loving and obeying, toward the present. Then take and label another photo so that today becomes part of the ongoing story of the journey you are on.

Don't!

Don't leave photographs that are stored in your computer out of the process.

How much?

£ To store photographs in pristine condition, acid-free products at www.my-history.co.uk start at £8.25 for an album and £6.50 for 100 sheets of paper. *Uncovering your Ancestry through Family Photographs* (Family Tree Books) costs £16.99.

This depends on the number of photographs, but will certainly take longer than you imagine as tales of significant people and events are retold.

 Who says?

Most things in life are moments of pleasure and a lifetime of embarrassment. Photography is a moment of embarrassment and a lifetime of pleasure.
Tony Benn, politician

 You are most likely to think

How did we persuade ourselves that those fashions looked good?

 You are least likely to think

These people should be forgotten.

To help you reflect

When the whole nation had finished crossing the Jordan, the Lord said to Joshua, 'Choose twelve men from among the people, one from each tribe, and tell them to take up twelve stones from the middle of the Jordan . . . and put them down at the place where you stay tonight . . . In the future, when your children ask you, "What do these stones mean?" tell them that the flow of the Jordan was cut off before the ark of the covenant of the Lord. When it crossed the Jordan, the waters of the Jordan were cut off. These stones are to be a memorial to the people of Israel forever' . . . And they are there to this day.
Joshua 4.1–3, 6–7, 9

I constantly remember you in my prayers . . . I have been reminded of your sincere faith, which first lived in your grandmother Lois and in your mother Eunice and, I am persuaded, now lives in you also. For this reason I remind you to fan into flame the gift of God.
2 Timothy 1.3–6

The date I labelled my photographs

A person or place I had forgotten was photographed

A photograph that recalls something that I treasure

What I will remember between here and heaven

33 Go to Africa

HOW? It would be possible to take a holiday in Africa in which you experience nothing different from any other resort in the world. (Some holidaymakers in Gambia, for instance, never need leave their hotel complex.) This is an unsatisfactory way of visiting Africa because, first, it gives little sense of a true African culture and, second, it robs the world's poorest continent of money that could be improving the local economy.

Companies that specialize in ethical tourism to Africa, such as Baobab (www.baobabtravel.com) work to ensure that the money tourists spend benefits local people, rather than international corporations, and minimizes damage to the environment. Most try to give visitors a less synthetic experience of African culture, and enhance their understanding of the history and civilization of the country as well as its astounding beauty and wildlife. *The Ethical Travel Guide* (Polly Pattullo, Earthscan Publications) includes a holiday directory compiled by Tourism Concern.

The development charity Tearfund has a programme called Transform that allows you to visit Africa and contribute to a project that alleviates poverty, instead of merely lamenting it. To find out about building, education or healthcare ventures, visit http://youth.tearfund.org/transform.

HOW EXTREME?

Here → ① ② ③ ④ **❺** → Heaven

What should I expect?

Nobody forgets visiting Africa. Its beauty is matchless and its ugliness shocking. For many people the overwhelming impression is of the contrast between wealth and poverty. It is the continent of safaris, sunshine, generosity and colour. It is also the continent of poverty, conflict, illness and unfulfilled potential. The unfair way in which trade takes place means that rich countries stay wealthy by keeping African communities poor. For some tourists their awareness of this is limited to being infuriated by beggars. Others return with a burning conviction that they should campaign for justice.

The centrality of faith (whether Christian or Muslim) to the lives of African people is a challenge to anyone who encounters it. To pray for the people of Africa is inevitable. To pray with the people of Africa is inspirational.

 Who says?

When the missionaries came to Africa they had the Bible and we had the land. They said, 'Let us pray.' We closed our eyes. When we opened them we had the Bible and they had the land.
Desmond Tutu, South African archbishop

How much?

£ Expect the economy class air fare from London to be between £500 and £800. Accommodation and activities that meet ethical standards typically add £90 per day to the price. *The Ethical Travel Guide* costs £12.99. Remember to account for the expense of medicines, visas, mosquito nets and other essentials.

🕐 The flight time from southern England to Addis Ababa (Ethiopia) is ten hours and to Maputo (Mozambique) 14 hours. Package holidays typically last between ten and 15 days. Tearfund's Transform programmes last from two weeks to four months.

Don't!

Don't think of Africa as if it were all one country. There are 54, each unique.

You are most likely to think

The only thing that is dark about this 'dark continent' is how ignorant I have been about it.

You are least likely to think

If only they could have what we have.

To help you reflect

The eunuch [from Ethiopia] asked Philip, 'Tell me, please, who is the prophet talking about, himself or someone else?' Then Philip began with that very passage of Scripture and told him the good news about Jesus. As they travelled along the road, they came to some water and the eunuch said, 'Look, here is water. Why shouldn't I be baptized?' . . . When they came up out of the water, the Spirit of the Lord suddenly took Philip away, and the eunuch did not see him again, but went on his way [to Africa] rejoicing.
Acts 8.34–36, 39

*If you do away with the yoke of oppression . . .
and if you spend yourselves in behalf of the hungry
and satisfy the needs of the oppressed,
then your light will rise in the darkness,
and your night will become like the noonday.
The Lord will guide you always;
he will satisfy your needs in a sun-scorched land
and will strengthen your frame.*
Isaiah 58.9–11

The dates of my visit to Africa

Which countries?

Adjectives that describe my impressions

What I will remember between here and heaven

34 Create a memorial

HOW? The many ways to create a lasting memorial to someone who has died include the following three.

Propose that a blue plaque is erected on a building in which the person lived. Email plaques@english-heritage.org.uk explaining why the person you nominate deserves to be remembered in this way (it should be someone who has made a 'positive contribution to human welfare or happiness'). Give biographical details and attach a photograph of the property to which the plaque could be attached. English Heritage receives about 100 suggestions every year, of which about three are successful. The scheme is strongest in London, but locations in other parts of England are considered. There is an equivalent scheme in Northern Ireland (www.ulsterhistory.co.uk).

Have a bench, on which is a plaque with the person's name, placed in a local park or cemetery. Almost all county councils have a scheme to allow this, and their websites give details and sometimes online application forms.

Create a memorial on the internet. Some memorial websites are rather sentimental, but www.relativesremembered.com allows you to post a photograph, write a celebration of someone's life and, if it is someone known personally to you, email friends to direct their attention to the site.

HOW EXTREME?

Here → ① ② ❸ ④ ⑤ → Heaven

What should I expect?

There are six billion people alive on the planet – that is more than have ever previously lived in its history. The living outnumber the dead. People of previous generations, especially those who had a Christian faith, wanted to be measured by their souls. For their loved-ones, the assurance of meeting again in eternal life was a sufficient memorial. However, society in this generation is shaped less by the certainty of resurrection, and for both secular and Christian people the need to remember someone in a distinctive way has become more important.

Creating a memorial gives you the opportunity to reflect on and take joy in the things that were unique about a person, whether it is someone famous or a friend. Working out why and where a person should be remembered involves focusing on the reasons the world is a better place because he or she has been in it. Take time to notice the names on plaques, and register that someone wanted to introduce those people to you. Creating a memorial announces to passers-by a deep Christian truth – that life (every life) is worth living.

Don't!

Don't propose yourself for a blue plaque because you need to have been dead for twenty years.

How much?

English Heritage bears the cost of a blue plaque. The price of a memorial bench varies, from £550 in West Lothian to £865 in Manchester. Posting a memorial at Relatives Remembered costs £10.

Two to five years pass between the proposal of a blue plaque and its unveiling. A memorial bench can be in place within four weeks. Online memorials can be read almost immediately.

Who says?

Reader, if you seek a memorial, look around you.
Christopher Wren, inscribed in St Paul's Cathedral, London, of which he was the architect, 1632–1723

You are most likely to think

When I meet this person in eternal life I will delight to tell them what I have done.

You are least likely to think

I am not worth remembering.

To help you reflect

The Lord says: 'To [those] . . . who choose what pleases me and hold fast to my covenant – to them I will give within my temple and its walls a memorial and a name better than sons and daughters; I will give them an everlasting name that will not be cut off.'
Isaiah 56.4, 5

Let us now sing the praises of famous men,
our ancestors in their generations . . .
Some of them have left behind a name,
so that others declare their praise.
But of others there is no memory;
they have perished as though they had never
*   existed . . .*
But these also were godly men,
whose righteous deeds have not been forgotten . . .
The assembly declares their wisdom,
and the congregation proclaims their praise.
Ecclesiasticus 44.1, 8–10, 15 (NRSV apocrypha)

The date I succeeded in creating a memorial

To whom, and where is it?

This is why I want the person to be remembered

What I will remember between here and heaven

69

35 Join a discussion group

HOW? Very many churches have discussion groups, either meeting weekly throughout the year or with members of other churches during a particular season (for example, Lent). Approach the leader of your local church and ask him or her to tell you what is on offer. Explain what you are looking for – either a group from diverse backgrounds and ages (to sharpen your mind), or one of people at similar life-stages (to share support). If all else fails, offer to start one.

There are published courses that encourage discussion about Christian experience, some requiring only the leader to have a copy, and others requiring every group member to write in their own. They are not essential, but they offer a structure. A good one will have introductory activities that put group members at their ease, Bible passages to read, questions that help you explore the Bible together, opportunities to share experience so that principles of the Christian faith become rooted in everyday experience of life, and ideas that capture the group's imagination to pray.

HOW EXTREME?

Here → **❶** ② ③ ④ ⑤ → Heaven

What should I expect?

A good discussion group (which usually means a good discussion group leader) allows you to expand your understanding of God by hearing him described in ways you haven't previously thought of. And it allows you to improve your life by hearing the stories of Christians who have had different experiences from you, encouraged by their faithfulness and strengthened by what they have learnt.

Don't feel compelled to say something about every subject, but equally don't arrive home feeling frustrated that your opinion went unheard. Listen, even when you disagree. Be aware that, through the voices and opinions of others, God may be speaking to you. And remember that he will teach you as much through the relationships that grow as through the ideas you discuss.

How much?

£ Group Bible study booklets vary greatly in cost between £3 and £9, but there are online resources available free of charge. Food and drink contribute to developing relationships in the group, and the cost could be shared.

🕐 Two hours weekly, preferably with a clear start and finish time.

Who says?

Imagine a group of people of all ages going on a long walk together. At times the children and adults will walk along together, talking as they go, sharing stories with first one person and then another, each observing different things and sharing their discoveries. At times the children lag behind, and the adults will have to urge them on. Sometimes the smallest children will asked to be carried. At other times, though, the children will dash ahead making new discoveries and may, perhaps, pull the adults along to see what they have found. For all there will be times of progress and times of rest and refreshment, time to admire the view, times of plodding on, and the eventual satisfaction of arriving at their destination.
Children in the Way, *a report to the Church of England's General Synod*

 You are most likely to think

Together we are more likely to understand God than we are as individuals.

 You are least likely to think

I have so much to teach the others.

Don't!

Don't forget that not all discussion groups have Christian subjects or members. A book club, meeting to discuss novels, is also a place where your understanding of God and life will grow if you allow it to. So is a local political party or a philosophy class.

To help you reflect

The believers sent Paul and Silas away to Berea. On arriving there, they went to the Jewish synagogue. Now the Bereans . . . received the message with great eagerness and examined the Scriptures every day to see if what Paul said was true.
Acts 17.10, 11

[In Ephesus] Paul . . . took the disciples with him and had discussions daily in the lecture hall of Tyrannus. This went on for two years, so that all the Jews and Greeks who lived in the province of Asia heard the word of the Lord.
Acts 19.9, 10

The date I joined a discussion group

The subject under discussion

The most interesting thing that was said

What I will remember between here and heaven

36 Experience nine lessons and carols

HOW? The best place in which to take part in a festival of nine lessons and carols is Kings College, Cambridge. The service has taken place there on the afternoon of Christmas Eve every year since 1918, and it has been broadcast live by the BBC since 1928. It is open to the public, but long queues form, and you need to be queuing by 10.30am to be confident of being admitted for the 3pm start.

Many churches worldwide replicate the pattern of alternating Bible readings with carols, some for a choir and some for the congregation. The services take place either on Christmas Eve or on the previous Sunday evening, often by candlelight. See local advertising to find details of a service in the neighbourhood, or contact churches that have a strong choral tradition.

HOW EXTREME?

Here → **①** ② ③ ④ ⑤ → Heaven

What should I expect?

The service uses nine short Bible readings to tell the story of the salvation of humankind from the beginnings of sin in the world, through God's promise to send the Messiah, to the birth of Jesus Christ in Bethlehem. Between the readings are carols, some sung by a choir and others for the congregation to join in. Traditionally the first of these is 'Once in Royal David's City' (the first verse sung as a solo by a young boy), and the last 'Hark the Herald Angels Sing'. There is no sermon, since the Bible is allowed to tell its own story. As its originators put it, 'The main theme is the development of the loving purposes of God . . . seen through the windows and words of the Bible.'

This is the most traditional means to rejoice in the decisive way in which God has intervened in human affairs. Because its format is unchanging as years go by, it allows you to gather up your accumulated memories of previous Christmases and bring their richness into the way you prepare to celebrate the day once more. No matter what may have changed in your life during the past year, this service remains unchanged – a reminder that the salvation of the world that approached its climax on the day Jesus was born was timeless, and will never falter or fail.

Instead of relaxing into the nostalgia of the familiar melodies, try to sing them as if you were happening on the words for the first time. Safe in the security of tradition, open yourself to being taken by surprise by the wonder of what it means for the almighty God to become a helpless infant.

How much?

 Nothing.

 80 to 90 minutes.

Don't!

Don't assume that it is compulsory to be jolly at Christmas. For those for whom Christmas brings to mind distressing memories, it is entirely acceptable to be quiet or sad. God honours that too.

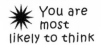 You are most likely to think

Now that I have been reminded of why we are celebrating, I am ready for Christmas to begin.

 You are least likely to think

I wish they'd done 'Rudolph the Red Nosed Reindeer'.

 Who says?

Beloved in Christ, at this Christmastide let it be our care and delight to hear again the message of the angels, and in heart and mind to go even unto Bethlehem and see this thing which is come to pass, and the babe lying in a manger.
E. W. Benson, Archbishop of Canterbury, 1829–1896 (traditionally the opening words of the service)

To help you reflect

The Word became flesh and made his dwelling among us. We have seen his glory, the glory of the One and Only, who came from the Father, full of grace and truth.
John 1.14

In the past God spoke to our forefathers through the prophets at many times and in various ways, but in these last days he has spoken to us by his Son, whom he appointed heir of all things, and through whom he made the universe. The Son is the radiance of God's glory and the exact representation of his being.
Hebrews 1.1–3

The date I took part in a service of nine lessons and carols

Where?

Which carol or reading spoke to me most of the meaning of Christmas?

What I will remember between here and heaven

37 Learn to sign

HOW? About 9 million people in the UK are hard of hearing, of whom about 700,000 are profoundly deaf. British Sign Language (BSL) is an elegant and fluent language used by up to 250,000 deaf and hearing people to aid their communication. It uses the hands, face and body expressively. Sign Supported English and Fingerspelling, which ponderously translate every spoken word and letter, are also in use.

The Council for the Advancement of Communication with Deaf People (www.cacdp.org.uk) offers information about ways of understanding issues that are unique to deaf people and improving communication. Click 'Find a course' at the top of the screen and follow the links to a map of Britain and Ireland showing where BSL can be learnt to a basic or advanced level. The online dictionary at www.britishsignlanguage.com has photographs of thousands of words and phrases, and is a good homework aid.

Deaf clubs are meeting places with social or sporting activities, and those who have been through a training course are often offered an introduction to their local club, where they can become more confident in the language by developing friendships.

HOW EXTREME?

Here → ① ② ③ ❹ ⑤ → Heaven

What should I expect?

Deafness is a cruel disability because it is hidden, and the difficulties of those who have hearing impediments are sometimes mistaken for a lack of intelligence. Entering witty, intellectual or gossipy conversation by signing dispels that very quickly. BSL is a language with its own beauty, slang and regional variations, just like Italian or Welsh. Its logic makes the vocabulary memorable, but it has a grammar distinct from spoken English. The sight of a church full of people enthusiastically praising God with every part of their bodies, but not one spoken word, is inspirational.

The visual nature of signing lends itself beautifully to conversations about everyday life, but there are fewer signs for the abstract theological words that sometimes feature in the way Christians talk. This means that discussions about God have to avoid clichés and be rephrased in ways that have real meaning about the ways faith adds value to daily life. Communicating in BSL can open your eyes to the difference God makes practically to the joys and difficulties of life, sometimes obscured by the language we use in worship. It really is the Word made flesh.

Don't!

Don't impose conversation on a deaf person if you are able to hear. Most deaf clubs welcome hearing people, but the custom is for deaf people to invite hearing people into their signed conversation, not the other way round.

BSL courses to level 1 cost from £195 at a local adult education college to £450 for an intensive business-related course. Taking the exam costs an additional £44. Fees for level 2 (more advanced) are about twice that.

A typical level 1 course is of 30 weekday evenings, or 15 full days.

You are most likely to think

Beyond sound, there are millions of ways in which God is communicating. Now I have encountered one more of them I see God clearer.

You are least likely to think

I give up. I'll just shout.

To help you reflect

'Bring my sons from afar
and my daughters from the ends of the earth –
everyone who is called by my name,
whom I created for my glory, whom I formed and
*   made.*
Lead out those who have eyes but are blind,
who have ears but are deaf . . .
You are my witnesses,' declares the Lord,
'and my servant whom I have chosen,
so that you may know and believe me.'
Isaiah 43.6–8, 10

Jesus commanded them not to tell anyone [about his miracles]. But the more he did so, the more they kept talking about it. People were overwhelmed with amazement. 'He has done everything well,' they said. 'He even makes the deaf hear and the mute speak.'
Mark 7.36, 37

Who says?

The problem is not that [deaf people] do not hear. The problem is that the hearing world does not listen.
Jesse Jackson, North American church leader and politician

The date I gained a qualification in BSL

My favourite word or phrase to sign

Names of some deaf people with whom I have had conversations

What I will remember between here and heaven

---

38 Ring bells

HOW? Find your local ringing society through the Central Council of Church Bell Ringers (click on 'With whom to ring' at www.cccbr.org.uk). Each county-wide society listed represents several local teams. 'Tower captains' take pleasure in passing on their skills to newcomers.

The English tradition of bellringing is unique. Elsewhere bells hang with the mouth down, and pulling a rope causes them to chime. However, English bellringing starts by raising the bell until the mouth is upward, resting against a wooden stay. When the rope is pulled, the bell travels through nearly 360 degrees. This gives more control over the moment at which the clapper strikes. The skill of bellringing is to make that happen at the right moment, and in a precise sequence.

The simplest sequence, 'Rounds', involves ringing all the bells in the tower (usually six or eight) in order from highest pitch to lowest: 123456. This is varied in thousands of ways by changing the order in which bells are rung. For instance, the order of the 'Plain Hunt' sequence is: 123456, 214365, 241635, 426153, 462513, 645231.

Many other 'methods' by which bells can be pealed are discussed in *The Ringing World*, which is both a weekly magazine and a website (www.ringingworld.co.uk), and computer software called Abel allows you to practise the changes.

HOW EXTREME?

Here → ① ② ❸ ④ ⑤ → Heaven

What should I expect?

Bellringing is a Christian service offered to enrich worship, just as singing in a choir is. It is part of a church's evangelism, reminding the community that worship is about to begin and inviting them to join. It is also part of a church's celebratory life, calling people to be exuberant in the way they rejoice at all God has done. And it encourages Christian fellowship, because bellringers are famously friendly.

Don't!

Don't give up after the first try, because almost everyone gets the hang of what initially appears complicated.

 Who says?

Ring out the old, ring in the new,
Ring, happy bells, across the snow:
The year is going, let him go;
Ring out the false, ring in the true . . .
Ring in the valiant man and free,
The larger heart, the kindlier hand;
Ring out the darkness of the land,
Ring in the Christ that is to be.
Alfred Lord Tennyson (from 'In Memoriam'), poet, 1809–1892

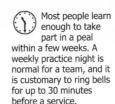

There is a tradition among bell ringers that beginners should be taught free. A nominal charge of about 30p covers expenses at practices, and travelling to different towers adds to the cost. However, wedding couples pay over £100 to have bells rung at their service, and that money may be used to cover the team's costs, or even to make payments to the ringers. An annual subscription to *The Ringing World* is £54, and the Abel computer program costs £20.

Most people learn enough to take part in a peal within a few weeks. A weekly practice night is normal for a team, and it is customary to ring bells for up to 30 minutes before a service.

To help you reflect

Make the robe of the ephod entirely of blue cloth . . . Make pomegranates of blue, purple and scarlet yarn around the hem of the robe, with gold bells between them . . . Aaron must wear it when he ministers. The sound of the bells will be heard when he enters the Holy Place before the Lord.
Exodus 28.31–35

You are most likely to think

I am part of an ancient and uniquely English tradition that involves both celebration and witness to the Church's presence in the community.

You are least likely to think

Hell's bells!

Then I looked, and there before me was the Lamb . . . I heard a sound from heaven like the roar of rushing waters and like a loud peal of thunder. The sound I heard was like that of harpists playing their harps. And they sang a new song . . . 'Fear God and give him glory, because the hour of his judgment has come. Worship him who made the heavens, the earth, the sea and the springs of water.'
Revelation 14.1–3, 7

The date I rang a peal of bells

At which church and with whom?

The name of the method

What I will remember between here and heaven

39 Gaze at the night sky

HOW? All you need are your eyes and a dark, cloudless sky. However, a chart or planisphere (a map with a moving part that reveals the changing appearance of the night sky) will increase your appreciation. In recent years, streetlights and illuminated buildings have dramatically reduced the visibility of the night sky from towns, so try to find an isolated (but safe) place.

The moon, with its shape appearing to change as the earth's shadow crosses it, is the most obvious feature. Star patterns, or constellations, that have legendary names such as Orion and Cassiopeia can be identified by picking out the more vivid stars among the millions of others. With the help of a star chart it is possible to identify the brighter planets that orbit our own sun.

At different times of the year, and at different latitudes, the appearance of the sky changes (for instance, a full moon that in the northern hemisphere has the appearance of a face, seems to show a silhouette of a rabbit from the southern hemisphere). Basic information about astronomy to enhance the experience can be found by visiting www.bbc.co.uk/sn and following the links to 'space'.

HOW EXTREME?

Here → **❶** ② ③ ④ ⑤ → Heaven

What should I expect?

Let your mind get lost in the impossible task of imagining the size of God's creation, as you consider the distance between you and the dots of light you can see. Then consider the detail of God's work – each star a sun around which planets circle, orbited by their own moons, of which God has detailed knowledge. As a sense of awe opens up within you, direct toward God the warmth you feel at being part of such a complex cosmos.

Go on to think about your place in God's creation. On planets millions of light years away, suns are rising and setting in majestic colours with no one to see them. Lucky you to have been created a human, able to appreciate beauty and wonder! The same God who is working on such a vast scale is intricately interested in the detail of your life. That is the measure of his love. Nothing you could say, sing or think comes close to expressing the greatness of God, but try your best anyway!

How much?

 A book of star charts or a planisphere each cost about £8.

Allow 15 minutes for your eyes to become attuned. Your vision will continue to improve for an hour, during which time your thoughts will expand too! If you live in a city, add time to reach a place without light pollution.

Don't!

Don't use an ordinary torch because it will impair what you can see in the sky. Instead, adapt one by wrapping red tissue paper or cellophane over the light.

 You are most likely to think

The time and scale of the project on which God is at work is breathtaking.

 You are least likely to think

The most important thing that has ever happened to the cosmos is me.

 Who says?

Question the beautiful earth, question the beautiful sea, question the beautiful air, amply spread everywhere. Question the beautiful sky, question the constellations of stars, question the sun making the day glorious with its brightness, question the moon tempering the darkness of the following night with its splendour . . . They all answer you, 'Take a look! We are beautiful.' Their beauty is their witness. Who made these beautiful, changeable things, if not the Great Unchanging Beauty?
Augustine, bishop of Hippo, 354–430

To help you reflect

When I consider your heavens, the work of your fingers,
the moon and the stars, which you have set in place,
what are mere mortals that you are mindful of them,
human beings that you care for them?
You made them a little lower than the heavenly beings
and crowned them with glory and honour.
Psalm 8.3–5

He determines the number of the stars and calls them each by name.
Great is our Lord and mighty in power; his understanding has no limit.
Psalm 147.4–5

	The date I gazed at the night sky

	Where?

	The impact it had on my understanding of God

	What I will remember between here and heaven

40 Pray the rosary

HOW? The rosary is a series of 80 prayers said in a particular order, often aloud, interspersed with meditation on Jesus' life. The best way to count how many prayers have been said is to move your fingers along a string of beads that has been developed over centuries for that purpose. The beads are in a circle, with gaps between them, and the circle has an attachment at the end of which is a cross.

Hold the cross and say the Apostles' Creed (a statement of what Christians believe). On the first large bead pray the Lord's Prayer. On the next three small beads, pray three Hail Marys (a prayer blessing the Virgin Mary and Jesus). At this point you will have worked up the attachment and will be on the circle. At the join, pray the Gloria (words of praise giving glory to God). Now take time to meditate on one of five events in Jesus' life (called mysteries). Over recent years the convention has emerged of considering his birth on Mondays and Saturdays, his ministry on Thursdays, his death on Tuesdays and Fridays, and the resurrection on Wednesdays and Sundays. During or after your meditation, pray the Lord's Prayer again as you hold the next large bead. On the following ten small beads, pray Hail Marys. On a gap between beads, hold the chain and pray the Gloria. That is the end of the first sequence (called a decade). Repeat the sequence four times to work your way round the whole set of rosary beads.

The words of all these prayers and mysteries can be found by following the links at www.catholic.org.uk.

HOW EXTREME?

Here → ① ❷ ③ ④ ⑤ → Heaven

What should I expect?

One of the reasons people find the rosary helpful is that it brings together discipline (praising God in a way that covers every part of our relationship with him) and liberty (letting your mind wander imaginatively through events in Jesus' life). To begin with, the process is unfamiliar and the prayers seem repetitive. However, in time it becomes possible to say the prayers from memory while your mind is set free to think about the five 'mysteries' that are set for the day.

Think of it like driving a car. To begin with the mechanics of driving occupy your entire attention, but in time they become so instinctive that you are free to think about the view and the conversation instead of what your feet and hands are doing. Similarly the rosary sets you free to think with gratitude and wonder about Jesus while the mechanics of repeating the prayers keep the activity disciplined.

How much?

💰 £5 to £20 for basic rosary beads, but jewelled ones can cost much more.

🕐 A rosary of five decades takes 20 minutes, or longer depending on how long you choose to meditate on Jesus' life.

Who says?

As your fingers count off the beads, you don't think about work or bills or school. Rather, you spend time with Christ.
Kevin Orlin Johnson, writing in Why Do Catholics Do That?

You are most likely to think

The discipline of touching the beads has stopped my mind wandering from giving unstinting worship to Jesus.

You are least likely to think

I don't know what to say when I pray.

Don't!

If you are not used to it, don't get over-anxious about mentioning Mary in your prayers. Like other characters in the Bible, there is much in her life to emulate. Sense her example helping you to worship her son Jesus, and use the words 'Hail Mary' in the same way that Gabriel did when he first said them to her (Luke 1.26–38).

To help you reflect

*I meditate on all your works
and consider what your hands have done.
I spread out my hands to you;
my soul thirsts for you like a parched land.
Answer me quickly, O Lord.
Psalm 143.5–7*

*Pray in the Spirit on all occasions with all kinds of prayers and requests. With this in mind, be alert and always keep on praying for all the saints.
Ephesians 6.18*

	The date I prayed the rosary

	A description of the beads I used

	Adjectives that describe the experience

	What I will remember between here and heaven

41 Keep a spiritual journal

HOW? Invest in a book that is colourful and beautifully bound, so that it will give this a sense of importance, and will be a pleasure to return to regularly. Either day by day or week by week, write a specialized diary. This is not just to keep a record of what has happened (although a brief summary of that will help you recall particular stages of your life when you revisit the book in years to come), but your personal response to spiritual matters.

Begin by writing the date. Imagine that Jesus is waiting outside the room, and that as soon as you have left he will come in and secretly read what you have written. What would you like to say to him?

Write quickly to record thoughts you have had about God and your place in the world. Document your feelings, doubts and discoveries. Particularly mention the impact that relationships, events and new ideas have on you. Note what and who you are praying for. Include Bible verses that register as significant, memories that resurface, and phrases from sermons, songs, books or television. As questions occur to you about your future, write them down as if you are having a conversation with yourself. Rebuke God when you need to. Paste in photographs or newspaper clippings if they make an impact on your emotions.

HOW EXTREME?

Here → ① ② ❸ ④ ⑤ → Heaven

What should I expect?

There are some benefits of keeping a spiritual journal that are immediate, and some that only emerge over a period of time. When you begin to write, you will discover that you know truths that you did not realize you knew. You will come to the end of each day or week with an enhanced sense of achievement, because expressing your inner life on paper will make small ideas seem significant. Even if you have to record negative thoughts, unburdening yourself of them allows God's compassion to begin healing them.

Coming back to entries after a year or more allows you to track the paths down which God has led you, and will reveal the progress you have made. Looking back at past hurts or crises and considering what they have subsequently allowed God to achieve in your life increases your confidence in trusting him for the future.

Don't!

Don't exaggerate or write in the hope of impressing someone. Be honest with yourself and God, and show no one else.

Be prepared to pay £8–£15 on a high quality book with blank pages.

Either 10–15 minutes per day or an hour per week. Only keeping a journal over a number of months or years will release its full value.

Who says?

A journal is a tool for self-discovery, an aid to concentration, a mirror for the soul, a place to generate and capture ideas, a safety valve for the emotions, a training ground for the writer, and a good friend and confidant.
Ron Klug, North American theologian

✳ You are most likely to think

I am learning what it means to live a worthwhile life. There is much that God needs to forgive, but over the course of time he is slowly preparing me for heaven.

☁ You are least likely to think

If my preparation for heaven is this slow I'll be dead before I get there.

To help you reflect

My son, do not forget my teaching, but keep my commands in your heart, for they will prolong your life many years and bring you prosperity. Let love and faithfulness never leave you; bind them around your neck, write them on the tablet of your heart. Then you will win favour and a good name in the sight of God and other people.
Proverbs 3.1–4

Remember those earlier days after you had received the light, when you stood your ground in a great contest in the face of suffering . . . because you knew that you yourselves had better and lasting possessions. So do not throw away your confidence; it will be richly rewarded. You need to persevere.
Hebrews 11.32–36

The date I began to keep a spiritual journal

What I intend to record in it

The frequency with which I have decided to write

What I will remember between here and heaven

42 See a cycle of mystery plays

HOW? Mystery plays tell the story of God's dealings with humankind from creation to the last judgement. Over 600 years old, they are the oldest kind of English theatre. They were performed in the open air – 30 short plays in one day. Each guild of craftsmen took responsibility for one episode (for example, the shipwrights acted the play of Noah's ark). They were performed on wagons, so crowds gathered at different locations and would stay there while one play after another was wheeled to them. There were costumes, scenery and special effects (such as firecrackers to make the mouth of hell scary).

The plays were performed annually between the 14th and the 16th centuries. Manuscripts of many still exist – four complete cycles named after the towns where they were performed (York, Chester, Wakefield and Coventry), and individual plays from other places. They were moving, musical, funny (a cantankerous Mrs Noah), and took liberties with the Bible (a sheep-stealing shepherd gets thwarted on his way to Bethlehem). They were also educational, telling the Christian story for an audience that could not read.

A revival of interest during the last 60 years means that they are now regularly performed, particularly in the towns where they originated. There are plans for open-air performances in Chester in 2008, and York in 2010. In other towns, such as Lichfield and Lincoln, productions take place every three or four years. They are often adapted and performed in indoor theatres as well.

HOW EXTREME?

Here → ① ② ❸ ④ ⑤ → Heaven

What should I expect?

Theatre began in England when the story of salvation burst out of the churches on to the streets. The solemnity of hearing the Bible read during a service was replaced by the colour, boisterousness and emotional power of the mystery plays. Because the message came in everyday language, it showed the burning relevance of Jesus' words to everyday life. It was entertaining, musical and tear-jerking. It made people excited about God.

Expect to become absorbed as the story unfolds, enjoying the fact that you are part of the centuries-old heritage of being British, and the aeons-old heritage of being human. Take friends who either never go to church, or never go to the theatre, or both. Ask yourself why churches can't make evangelism this exhilarating.

Professional productions reflect theatre prices and vary from £10 to £40. The York cycle is free as it progresses through the streets, but premium seats are reserved at a cost.

 Modern productions present only a selection of the plays (although a performance of a complete cycle in Toronto in 1998 lasted from 6am to midnight). The plays are usually presented in two-hour versions, but productions in the spirit of the original, such as the York cycle, last up to six hours.

Don't!

Don't moan if some colourful details of the plays are not the same as the Bible text.

 You are most likely to think

This story will never lose its power, century after century.

 Who says?

A dazzling South African version of the medieval Chester mystery plays . . . Why at the end did the audience leap to its feet? . . . I believe the audience is responding to the power of the original plays and their retelling of the Christian story from the creation to the crucifixion and resurrection. Even in a secular age, we find a mythical resonance in the . . . story of betrayal, redemption and rebirth.
Michael Billington, in the Guardian, *reviewing a production available on DVD from Heritage Theatre Productions, entitled* The Mysteries (Yiimimangaliso)

 You are least likely to think

Heard it all before!

To help you reflect

I will open my mouth in parables,
I will utter hidden things, things from of old . . .
what our fathers have told us . . .
so the next generation would know them,
even the children yet to be born,
and they in turn would tell their children.
Psalm 78.2, 3, 6, 7

Pray for us, that God may open a door for our message, so that we may proclaim the mystery of Christ.
Colossians 4.3

The date I saw a mystery play cycle

Where? And what was the style?

The most memorable scene

What I will remember between here and heaven

43 Plant a tree

HOW? Buy a sapling at a garden centre or online. Choose a location at least ten metres from buildings, and a tree that is appropriate to the the space (perhaps a beech in a large garden or a wild cherry in a smaller one). Soak the roots of the tree. Dig a hole deep enough for the junction between the root and the stem to be at ground level when it is filled in. One person should hold the tree, shaking it gently so that the soil trickles through and around the roots as another person spades it in. Tread the soil firmly around the roots and water it well. Instructions designed to encourage children to participate can be found at www.treeforall.co.uk.

If a suitable space is not available, several schemes allow trees to be planted on your behalf in the UK or in the developing world. Through Forests for Life, trees can be planted in memory of someone or to mark the birth of a baby who will grow alongside it.

HOW EXTREME?

Here → ① ② ❸ ④ ⑤ → Heaven

What should I expect?

Planting a tree is a determined act of faith that there will be a future for life on this planet after your own death, and for as long as God chooses to sustain his plan for humankind. It is a matter of simple generosity.

It is generous because it reverses the disastrous extent of carbon emissions, with their contribution to global warming, to which we contribute every time we use fuel. Trees recycle carbon dioxide into oxygen. Planting trees is an affirmation that the life of generations to come is more important than the lazy comfort of the generation that is presently alive. It may be done out of guilt at a wasteful lifestyle or out of a positive attempt to reverse an unsustainable trend – both speak of the repentance to which all the Bible's prophets call us.

It is also generous because others will enjoy the full benefit of the investment you are making, not you. Someone else's children will see the full-grown tree that you can only imagine. War, disease or someone's whim could prevent it, but planting a tree despite the possibility of that happening is a statement that hope is a better way of life than cynicism. In that respect, it is an active prayer for the future of the place in which you have planted and the souls who will one day tread the paths you have trod.

Don't!

Don't plant leylandii in a small suburban garden, because they grow so fast that they block the light and view of neighbours.

How much?

A sapling suitable for a garden costs £20 to £60, depending on the species. At www.forests4life.com it is possible to sponsor the planting of a tree in English woodland for £42.30. Projects to protect the rain forest in South America ask for donations of £25 per acre at www.worldlandtrust.org.

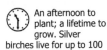

An afternoon to plant; a lifetime to grow. Silver birches live for up to 100 years; ashes twice that.

Who says?

Trees are the earth's endless effort to speak to the listening heaven.
Rabindranath Tagore, poet, 1861–1941

You are most likely to think

One day in the future someone still unborn will sit in the shade of this tree and be glad of what I have done.

You are least likely to think

I fancy a bonfire. How long until Guy Fawkes night?

To help you reflect

Be not afraid, O wild animals, for the open pastures are becoming green. The trees are bearing their fruit; the fig tree and the vine yield their riches. Be glad, O people of Zion, rejoice in the Lord your God, for he has given you the autumn rains in righteousness.
Joel 2.22, 23

The angel showed me the river of the water of life, as clear as crystal, flowing from the throne of God . . . On each side of the river stood the tree of life, bearing twelve crops of fruit, yielding its fruit every month. And the leaves of the tree are for the healing of the nations.
Revelation 22.1, 2

The date I planted a tree

Where and what?

A message to people who will see the full-grown tree

What I will remember between here and heaven

44 Wash feet

HOW? Some churches have services of foot washing on the Thursday before Easter (Maundy Thursday). During the service the leaders of the church, following the example of Jesus, wash the feet of some or all of the congregation. This symbolic action requires the leaders to kneel humbly in front of people they lead with a bowl of warm water and a towel. A handful of water is poured over just one foot, which is then dried. In variations of this pattern, sometimes each member of the congregation washes the feet of a neighbour – usually men serving men and women serving women. It is almost always followed by communion.

Telephone the offices of local churches as Easter approaches and ask whether they know of a service locally at which this will feature.

HOW EXTREME?

Here → ① **❷** ③ ④ ⑤ → Heaven

What should I expect?

In the time of Jesus foot washing was a courtesy to guests who arrived at your house having walked through dusty streets in open sandals. It was the slightly unpleasant task of a slave. The night before he died, Jesus put himself in the place of a slave by washing the feet of his embarrassed followers. His intention was to give a radically different model of leadership that is expressed through humility, rather than expecting deference.

The tradition of washing feet in Christian worship dates back to the 2nd century. It is a reminder to congregations that leaders are there not to be served, but to serve. It is a humbling experience for the person who washes the feet, but it is equally moving for the people whose feet are washed, since it requires them to walk barefoot and vulnerable among friends and strangers.

Until 1688, kings and queens of the UK marked Maundy Thursday by washing the feet of destitute people, but after James II the practice was replaced by distributing ceremonial money to representatives of charities.

Expect to feel challenged by God about your place in the community, and whether you have been held back from giving others the help they need by pride or embarrassment. It is also a time to reflect that we sometimes feel unable to ask for help because that suggests weakness, and to be aware that although that is the way of the world, it has no place in Christian experience.

How much?

 Nothing.

 A foot washing service lasts up to 90 minutes.

Don't!

Don't arrive with feet that actually do need washing. This should remind everyone of the need for humility, not hygiene.

Who says?

Lord of eternity dwells in
   humanity,
kneels in humility and
   washes our feet.
O what a mystery,
   meekness and majesty,
bow down and worship for
   this is your God.
*Graham Kendrick,
composer, from the hymn
'Meekness and majesty'*

You are most likely to think

Why do I keep buying more and more shoes when I only have one pair of feet?

You are least likely to think

A mark of how successful your life has been is never having to ask anyone for help.

To help you reflect

Jesus knew that the Father had put all things under his power, and that he had come from God and was returning to God; so he got up from the meal, took off his outer clothing, and wrapped a towel around his waist. After that, he poured water into a basin and began to wash his disciples' feet, drying them with the towel that was wrapped around him.
John 13.3–5

[Jesus] turned toward the woman and said to Simon, 'Do you see this woman? I came into your house. You did not give me any water for my feet, but she wet my feet with her tears and wiped them with her hair. You did not give me a kiss, but this woman, from the time I entered, has not stopped kissing my feet. You did not put oil on my head, but she has poured perfume on my feet. Therefore, I tell you, her many sins have been forgiven – for she loved much.'
Luke 7.44–47

The date I took part in a foot washing service

Where?

Name of the person whose feet I washed, or who washed mine

What I will remember between here and heaven

89

45 Tell someone what you believe

HOW? More than in any previous generation, people are very interested to know what you believe about God. The obstacle is not finding an opportunity, but being able to say something worthwhile when an occasion arises, so it is sensible to have thought in advance about what you would like to say in these circumstances.

All Christians believe three things that distinguish them from anyone else. First, there is a God. Second, in some way too complex for human minds fully to grasp, God was uniquely present on earth two thousand years ago in the person of Jesus Christ. And third, that matters!

Without preparing a speech, have in mind some things you could say about each of those three things. First, why have you come to the conclusion that there is a God who created and cares for the world, rather than believing the cosmos is here by chance? For instance, does the splendour of nature persuade you, or the existence of love, or the beauty of music? Second, what do you find so compelling about Jesus that you want to be like him? Is it his personality, his teaching, his challenge, or what you read in the Bible of his power? Third, what positive difference does it make to your life to have it shaped by those things? How has it made your life better to know that God is with you, and that Christian people surround you, through good times, bad times, or just ordinary times?

HOW EXTREME?

Here → ① ❷ ③ ④ ⑤ → Heaven

What should I expect?

It is what you say about the third thing Christians believe that people will find most persuasive. We live in an age in which most people find arguing over the question, 'Is it true?' to be a negative experience. (They associate it, rightly or wrongly, with the violence and hatred that religion has caused.) However, they are extremely interested in the question, 'Does it work?' And when they discover that following Jesus has made you a better, happier, more fulfilled person, they find that compelling.

Make friends naturally with all kinds of people – at parties, at work, through sport, in and around schools. There is no need to manipulate occasions to talk to them about your faith; let opportunities arise naturally. For instance, when colleagues ask you on a Monday morning, 'What did you do yesterday?' tell them that you went to church. Then wait for them to ask you more about it, as days or weeks later they surely will.

As well as telling people about your Christian faith, ask what they believe, and take as much interest in it as they do in what you say. As the conversation develops, enjoy it and chat naturally. There is no need to resort to religious phrases or theological explanations. Leave those to the preachers!

Nothing.

 This one could run and run.

 You are most likely to think

The world has a little more good news in it than it did yesterday.

 You are least likely to think

He or she must think I'm a fool.

How much?

Don't!

Don't get into an argument, or tell someone that they ought to believe the same things that you do.

Who says?

Evangelism is no more than one beggar telling another where to find bread.
D.T. Niles, Sri Lankan theologian and president of the World Council of Churches, 1908–1970

To help you reflect

Always be prepared to give an answer to everyone who asks you to give the reason for the hope that you have. But do this with gentleness and respect.
1 Peter 3.15

[Paul wrote:] Pray for us, too, that God may open a door for our message, so that we may proclaim the mystery of Christ, for which I am in chains. Pray that I may proclaim it clearly, as I should. Be wise in the way you act toward outsiders; make the most of every opportunity. Let your conversation be always full of grace, seasoned with salt, so that you may know how to answer everyone.
Colossians 4.3–6

The date I told someone what I believe

Who?

What was their reaction?

 What I will remember between here and heaven

46 Stand for election

HOW? To be a candidate in a local government election you must be over 21 and a citizen of the UK, the EU or the Commonwealth. For a parliamentary election you must be a British, Irish or Commonwealth citizen. Local councillors need to have home or work connections with the area, and may not be bankrupt.

Two months before election day, the council publishes a Notice of Election on its website, notice boards and in local newspapers. It explains the process, the timetable and the person to contact (the Electoral Services Officer). You will need signatures from ten supporters who live in the ward in which you intend to stand. Peter Arnold's book *How to be a Local Councillor* is a practical guide, and the fact sheets at www.electoralcommission.org.uk are exhaustive (click 'Publications' on the right of the screen).

Thousands of councillors are independent. However, it is also possible to represent a political party, where a support structure is in place to help contest elections. For this, you need to contact the local branch of the party and, if you are interviewed and selected, complete an authorization form.

There are many other ways of offering yourself for election to an office in which you can influence society for good. Stand as a trade union shop steward, a school governor, a church council member, a deacon, or an official of a residents' association, student union or youth parliament. Christian Action, Research and Education has details of what it means to be involved in public life at its website www.changeactivist.org.uk (click 'Take action').

HOW EXTREME?

Here → ① ② ③ ④ ❺ → Heaven

What should I expect?

By standing for election you risk rejection. You have an opportunity to use your ideas, personality and influence for good, but you also make yourself vulnerable to the possibility that someone else's skills are preferred. If you are entering the election with the intention of being a servant, you will be open with God about your usefulness to him. However, if you have your own interests at heart, rejection will sting.

The essence of democracy is that people serve people, instead of dominating people, and entering that process allows you to be God's representative, witnessing by what you say and do that the values of his Kingdom have true worth.

How much? There is no charge to contest most elections. However, candidates for the UK parliament pay a deposit of £500, which is refunded unless you poll less than 5 per cent of the votes. *How to be a Local Councillor* (How To Books) costs £8.99.

 A survey of councillors in Devon showed the average time commitment to be 33 hours per week. In the run up to an election the number of hours is greater. Other public offices demand less time, but none are effortless.

Don't!

Don't give up if you are unsuccessful the first time. People become more inclined to vote for you as you become familiar.

 You are most likely to think

I am here to bring goodness out of this situation, just as salt brings the taste out of food.

 You are least likely to think

What's in it for me?

 Who says?

I can't see any future for a church that doesn't accept that it must be involved in the part of [God's world] which is political and economic. A church which claims that the world is for Christ must be up to its neck in politics.
Lord Donald Soper, Methodist leader, 1903–1998

To help you reflect

The one in authority is God's servant to do you good . . . Submit to the authorities, not only because of possible punishment but also because of conscience.
Romans 13.4–5

Do not forget to do good and to share with others, for with such sacrifices God is pleased. Obey your leaders and submit to their authority. They keep watch over you as those who must give an account. Obey them so that their work will be a joy, not a burden, for that would be of no advantage to you.
Hebrews 13.16, 17

	The date I stood for election
	The post for which I stood
	The result of the election
	What I will remember between here and heaven

47 Take a new route to work

HOW? Get off the bus one stop early and walk the rest of the distance. Or one stop late. Travel in the front carriage of a train instead of the back one. Jog instead of walking. Or turn left where you usually turn right and take a long cut. Share a car journey. Climb six flights of stairs instead of taking the lift. Or use the ramp for wheelchair users instead of the stairs.

If you work in your own home, create an equivalent variation on your routine. Eat breakfast before you shower, or vice versa. Make yourself up to look stunning even though the only person who will see it is the baby. Get dressed listening to a different radio station. Or in silence!

HOW EXTREME?

Here → ❶ ② ③ ④ ⑤ → Heaven

What should I expect?

Be acutely aware of what you are doing, what you observe and how you feel. For some, it will be a positive experience. They will notice details they had not seen before (for example, a house where the dustbin is kept in a more logical place, a plant that is in flower at an unexpected time). They will discover shops they did not know were there, or be intrigued to perceive how the area seems different to someone pushing a buggy, riding a bicycle, or partially sighted. Others will find themselves irritated by the disruption to their routine, feeling that their time has been wasted, and that the new thoughts they have had are too insubstantial to have been worth the effort. Either will interrupt the usual patterns of your brain, and stimulate it to view other things in innovative ways.

We have a God who lives in a constant present, endlessly thinking new thoughts, and constantly reinventing the way it is sustained in order to bring good out of confusion and love out of coincidence. Every new route for you becomes a new opportunity for him. With your eyes open to what he has to show you, your head will become open to what he might teach you, and your heart to the desire to align yourself with God's plan for the world.

How much?

💷 Altering your mode of transport may increase the expense. (However, it may decrease it!)

🕐 Allow extra time, even if you anticipate a short cut.

94

Don't!

Don't stop there! Eat lunch in a new place or at a different time, use the toilet on a different level, drink water instead of coffee, speak to a different colleague, rearrange your desk, change your computer screensaver, give customers their change with your left hand instead of your right, subtly change your form of words when you answer the telephone so that you sound more cheerful.

 ## Who says?

If you're not spending every single waking moment of your life radically rethinking the nature of the world, then you're wasting your day.
Douglas Coupland, novelist

To help you reflect

Paul and his companions travelled throughout the region of Phrygia and Galatia, having been kept by the Holy Spirit from preaching the word in the province of Asia. When they came to the border of Mysia, they tried to enter Bithynia, but the Spirit of Jesus would not allow them to. So they passed by Mysia and went down to Troas. During the night Paul had a vision of a man of Macedonia standing and begging him, 'Come over to Macedonia and help us.' After Paul had seen the vision, we got ready at once to leave for Macedonia, concluding that God had called us to preach the gospel to them.
Acts 16.6–10

[The Lord declares:]
'I will lead the blind by ways they have not known,
along unfamiliar paths I will guide them;
I will turn the darkness into light before them
and make the rough places smooth.
These are the things I will do;
I will not forsake them.'
Isaiah 42.16

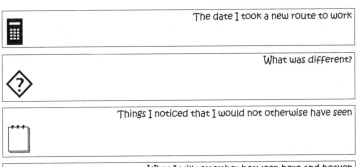

The date I took a new route to work

What was different?

Things I noticed that I would not otherwise have seen

What I will remember between here and heaven

48 Walk the stations of the cross

HOW? Pilgrims visiting Jerusalem have, since the earliest days of Christianity, traced the route along which Jesus staggered carrying his cross to the execution site. It is known as the *Via Dolorosa* ('the grief-stricken way'). Walking the route was popularized during the 14th century by the Franciscan monks who were given custody of the sites associated with Jesus' life. Franciscans still lead a pilgrimage through the Jerusalem streets every Friday, starting at St Stephen's Gate at 3p.m. and stopping to pray at the presumed locations of particular events.

As pilgrims returned, thrilled by what they had seen in Jerusalem, churches responded by bringing Jerusalem to those who could not travel. They commissioned paintings and sculptures, placed at intervals either indoors or outdoors, to tell the story of Jesus' journey to Calvary, and encouraged people to walk along the sequence meditating on his suffering. By the 18th century the number was fixed at 14 – eight events recorded in the gospels and six from Christian legends. In recent years Pope John Paul II devised a new sequence using biblical events only, and a fifteenth is often added to mark Jesus' resurrection.

Today almost all Roman Catholic places of worship and a few Protestant churches have artwork of some kind to allow people to walk the stations of the cross. There is no set form of words to pray, although many churches provide extracts from Scripture to aid meditation, and there are occasions (Good Friday for instance) when services are held in which a whole congregation walks together. The internet also has sequences of stations of the cross, and www.liturgies.net/Lent/Stations/Stations.htm is a portal to the best.

HOW EXTREME?

Here → ① ❷ ③ ④ ⑤ → Heaven

What should I expect?

Although the internet sites are beautiful and moving, the true value of doing this is as much the walk as the stations. As Jesus is seen to move along the grief-stricken way, so you are moving with him. Realize that you are walking the way of Christ to the very end, just as he will walk with you through life no matter how difficult or lonely that journey becomes.

Stop at each station. Put your weight equally on both feet to relax yourself in front of it. Look first at the artwork and try to understand what the artist has done to portray the dread of the event. Then read the scripture that sheds light on the story. Contemplate the fact that what is taking place in the carving or picture brought about the salvation of humankind. Your salvation! Pray with quiet reverence, making Jesus the centre of your prayer – in thanks, in devotion, or just in sorrow that the world was and still is capable of doing something so wicked.

How much?

Nothing (although if you intend to visit the actual sites, air fares to Jerusalem start at £250).

Walking the stations of the cross in a church takes at least an hour. The procession in Jerusalem lasts about three hours.

 You are most likely to think

All this for me!

 You are least likely to think

It was not worth doing because it isn't historically accurate.

Don't!

Don't finish your meditation with Jesus dead. Rejoice about the fundamental truth of the Christian faith – that he lives.

To help you reflect

Christ suffered for you, leaving you an example, that you should follow in his steps. 'He committed no sin, and no deceit was found in his mouth.' When they hurled their insults at him, he did not retaliate; when he suffered, he made no threats . . . By his wounds you have been healed.
1 Peter 2.21–24

Is it nothing to you, all you who pass by? Look around and see. Is any suffering like the suffering that was inflicted on me?
Lamentations 1.12

 Who says?

We adore you, O Christ, and we bless you, because by your holy cross, you have redeemed the world. *Francis of Assisi, founder of the Franciscan order, 1182–1226, words that are used by tradition at every station*

The date I walked the stations of the cross

Where, and what was the style of the images?

The station that touched me in a new way

What I will remember between here and heaven

49 Contribute to the Wikipedia

HOW? The Wikipedia is a vast encyclopaedia on the internet. Uniquely, it is free and accessible to anyone. It is written entirely by volunteers, and anyone in the world can contribute from their own expertise. It not only has an encyclopaedia, but also the texts of history's most important books, speeches and quotations. In the few years since it was founded in 2001, it has become the most knowledgeable thing on the planet and is among the 30 most visited websites. It can be found at www.wikipedia.org.

Not only can anyone read the Wikipedia, anyone can contribute to it. Next to each of the three million articles is a tab to click if you wish to add information, or correct something inaccurate. It is also possible to post an article about a new subject, but this requires you to register. Full instructions appear in the Wikipedia FAQs. An army of volunteers collaborates to develop it and guard against its abuse.

Before a full article is written, a brief paragraph (called a 'stub') is posted, with an invitation to anyone with expertise or the ability to research the subject to expand it. Tens of thousands of these are waiting for attention. Browse them, find one about which you have information to add, edit it and post it. If you do not know where to start, there are nearly 1,000 stubs related to Christianity alone. To find them, click on 'Categories' in the middle of the main page, then on 'Christianity' in the Religions section, and finally on 'Christianity stubs' which is listed under S in the alphabetical list.

HOW EXTREME?

Here → ① ② ❸ ④ ⑤ → Heaven

What should I expect?

The Wikipedia has critics who point out that it is open to vandalism and each article is only as reliable as its last editor. While this is true, it is remarkable how little abuse happens. The desire to do good is genuinely defeating the desire to do harm.

The shared ideology of the Wikipedia community, that education should be freely available to every human being, is one of the few surviving remnants of the idealism of the internet's founding fathers, before it was overwhelmed by pornography and spam. It is self-regulating and self-healing. It also echoes the idealism of the first Christians in Jerusalem who sold their property and pooled their resources for the good of them all (although that too was vulnerable to trust being destroyed by a couple of selfish people). Contributing to the Wikipedia involves you in one of the greatest glories of the free world.

H o w   m u c h ?

Free. Gloriously and everlastingly free!

If you wanted to read it all, you would have had to start before the birth of Jesus. The editing process is instant, but the time commitment depends on your knowledge and devotion and could become huge.

✳ You are most likely to think

All the knowledge in God's world should be available to all the people of God's world.

☁ You are least likely to think

It's not what you know; it's who you know.

Don't!

Don't bluff, because you will be found out. If you do so maliciously you will be blocked.

Who says?

I'm doing this for the child in Africa who is going to use free textbooks and reference works produced by our community and find a solution to the crushing poverty that surrounds him . . . And I'm doing this for my own daughter, whom I hope will grow up in a world where culture is free, not proprietary, and where control of knowledge is in the hands of people everywhere [without needing to ask] permission from anyone. *Jimmy Wales, founder of the Wikipedia*

To help you reflect

Wisdom is a shelter as money is a shelter, but the advantage of knowledge is this: that wisdom preserves the life of its possessor. Consider what God has done!
Ecclesiastes 7.12–13

Paul, a servant of God and an apostle of Jesus Christ for the faith of God's elect and the knowledge of the truth that leads to godliness –
a faith and knowledge resting on the hope of eternal life.
Titus 1.1, 2

	The date I contributed to the Wikipedia

	What subject?

	Something I have added to the world's accumulated knowledge

	What I will remember between here and heaven

50 Find out about Islam

HOW? The Islamic Information Centre helps people go beyond a cursory knowledge. Visit www.islamicinformationcentre.co.uk for details of video resources, as well as books that can be read online (click on 'What do Muslims believe?' in the resources section). *Islam, a Very Short Introduction* (Malise Ruthven, Oxford Paperbacks) requires concentration, but is rewarding. The Qur'an (Koran) is a much more complex book than the Bible and without a commentary you will be tempted to give up. Begin with *The Essential Koran: The Heart of Islam – A Selection of Introductory Readings*, Thomas Cleary, HarperCollins.

Mosques vary between those which are geared up to welcome and inform non-Muslim guests (for instance, the mosque in Edinburgh), and those that regard visitors with polite caution. Make local enquiries using telephone numbers from www.muslimdirectory.co.uk.

HOW EXTREME?

Here → ① ② ❸ ④ ⑤ → Heaven

What should I expect?

Expect to discover that the values at the heart of Islam are loving, charitable and godly. About one billion people worldwide follow the teachings of Muhammad, who lived in the Middle East from 570 until 633. They are preserved in the Qur'an, written (and only valid) in Arabic following revelations to Muhammad from God, known by the name Allah.

According to Islam, there is only one God, who is our creator, sustainer, guide and judge. It is the task of all humans to make the world a better place, and they do that by going beyond their natural inclination to selfishness. A series of prophets have revealed this to humankind through the ages. Muslims recognize Jesus as one of the most important (although they do not worship him as God), but the last and greatest is Muhammad, who is profoundly revered.

Five essential duties of all Muslims ('Pillars of Faith') are to proclaim that: 'There is no God but Allah, and Muhammad is his prophet', to face Mecca and pray five times daily, to be generous to the poor, to fast from dawn until sunset throughout the month of Ramadan (mid-Autumn in the UK), and to make a pilgrimage to Mecca (Muhammad's birthplace).

Don't!

Don't try to persuade yourself that Islam and Christianity are identical in all but name, but do recognize that Muslims are praying to the same God that Abraham and Jesus prayed to, and should have friendship, understanding and respect.

Islam, a Very Short Introduction costs £6.99 and *The Essential Koran* £8.59. The text of the Qur'an in an English translation can be read free online at www.quran.org.uk. If you visit a mosque, make a donation to its ministry among poor people.

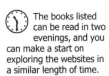

The books listed can be read in two evenings, and you can make a start on exploring the websites in a similar length of time.

Who says?

Jesus came with manifest proofs. He said, 'Now I have come to you with wisdom. I will resolve for you some of the things about which you differ. Therefore, worship Allah, and obey my commands. This is the right way.'
Holy Qur'an 43.62, 63

You are most likely to think

All Christians ought to learn these things in order to diminish fear and promote peace.

You are least likely to think

I am full of hate.

To help you reflect

God, who made the world and everything in it, is the Lord of heaven and earth and does not live in temples built by hands. And he is not served by human hands, as if he needed anything, because he himself gives all life and breath and everything else. From one man he made all the nations, that they should inhabit the whole earth . . . God did this so that they would seek him and perhaps reach out for him and find him, though he is not far from each one of us.
Acts 17.24–27

The Lord said to [Abraham] . . .
'I will make you into a great nation and I will bless you;
I will make your name great, and you will be a blessing.
I will bless those who bless you, and whoever curses you I will curse;
and all peoples on earth will be blessed through you.'
Genesis 12.1–3

The date I found out about Islam

How?

Something I learnt that changed me

What I will remember between here and heaven

51 Forgive a wrong

HOW? This requires an act of will, rather than making an emotional decision. It is not like a contract between you and the person who has wronged you which requires him or her to do something in exchange. In fact, the other person doesn't even need to know that they have been forgiven. You need simply to decide that you are no longer going to let the wrong that has been done to you have a hold over you. You don't need to have the last word in an argument. You don't need to have got what you deserved (in fact, you probably haven't). You just need to let go.

The question of whether you tell the other person they are forgiven needs to be taken carefully. It may reopen aggravation and create yet another sin that needs to be forgiven. Alternatively, it may re-establish a relationship that will bring you both happiness. Or it may be that you can no longer contact the person anyway. Make a choice, and decide in advance not to let the consequences spoil the joy of having released yourself from the burden.

HOW EXTREME?

Here → ① ② ❸ ④ ⑤ → Heaven

What should I expect?

You are not doing this for the benefit of the person who has wronged you. You are doing it to improve your own life. Of course, the side effect may be that the other person's situation improves too. It is possible that some of the ordinary joys of friendship may open up again for them. But the main point of forgiving a wrong is that you can be released from the power it has over you.

After forgiving someone, you are no longer a victim. You have done something about the wrong that only you could do, and the person who inflicted it has no power to stop you. A burden will lift. Back in control of the situation you will discover that what the Bible says about the Kingdom of God is true – in weakness there is a great strength.

You are treading a route that Jesus took when, with his dying breath, he chose to forgive his murderers. God did not begin to work the resurrection when the women arrived on the Sunday; he began it when the wrongdoing was forgiven on the Friday.

How much?

Nothing

An instant, so long as you never reopen the old sores.

Don't!

Don't attach conditions, because if you constantly have to monitor whether the conditions are being fulfilled you will not be free of the burden.

 You are most likely to think

I have got nothing to lose. If it doesn't work, I can always go back to the hate and tension again. But I just don't want to.

 You are least likely to think

Obviously there is nothing about me that needs to be forgiven.

 Who says?

God has brought us to this moment and I just want to say to you: I cannot, when someone says, 'Forgive me,' reply, 'I do not.'
Desmond Tutu, South African archbishop, responding to the repentance of the Dutch Reformed Church for the part it had played in maintaining apartheid (the national policy of enforced separation of people of different races)

To help you reflect

[Jesus said,] 'Be merciful, just as your Father is merciful. Do not judge, and you will not be judged. Do not condemn, and you will not be condemned. Forgive, and you will be forgiven. Give, and it will be given to you. A good measure, pressed down, shaken together and running over, will be poured into your lap. For with the measure you use, it will be measured to you.'
Luke 6.36–38

Bear with each other and forgive whatever grievances you may have against one another. Forgive as the Lord forgave you. And over all these virtues put on love, which binds them all together in perfect unity. Let the peace of Christ rule in your hearts, since as members of one body you were called to peace.
Colossians 3.13–15

	The date I forgave a wrong

	Draw a symbol that will remind only you who or what was involved

	What difference has it made to the relationship?

	What I will remember between here and heaven

52 Attempt an extreme sport

HOW? Extreme sports feature acute speed, height, danger or spectacular stunts. Mountain biking sees you negotiating a course of natural and man-made obstacles. Parkour is 'free running' over an urban landscape in leaps and bounds. Snowboarding takes skiing to its acrobatic limits. White-water rafting pits a team in a boat against river rapids. And there are many ingenious ways to throw yourself from a great height, of which bungee jumping is the most popular and skydiving the most intense.

Television's Extreme Sports Channel (www.extreme.com) is the place to get inspiration and www.extremelives.co.uk is the place to get tuition.

Here → ① ② ③ ④ ❺ → Heaven

What should I expect?

Traditional sports bring out qualities of commitment and fair play, but extreme sports offer a more individual challenge. You create your own goals and the constraints are not the rules and referees, but your own courage and ability. You discover your limits, bear the consequences of your own actions, and the objective is to overtake yourself.

As in spiritual life, it is impossible to see the worth of these sports by observing; only participation counts. You can experience a rush of adrenaline by taking part in a safe environment – such as skydiving in tandem, harnessed to an instructor who makes sure nothing goes wrong. That provides a momentary escape from life. However, enthusiasts of extreme sports scorn half-measures and put themselves to the test. It is an opportunity to stop life escaping them.

A feeling that we should be pushing ourselves more is lodged deeply in our inner lives. Extreme sports provide a way to aspire to something that cannot be delivered to your armchair, and the result is a greater appreciation of your own body, the natural environment, and the potential that God has placed in you.

Who says?

We are simply a group of guys that are passionate about riding, faith and living that faith [in Christ]. That's the bottom line. We believe that everybody has faith – whether you are doing a sixty feet huck, racing downhill or back flipping. Not only do these things take balls of steel and heaps of skill, but they take faith. A faith that is not always easily recognizable and sometimes impossible to touch – but it is there. *Will New, founder of extreme sports organization Rezurgence*

How much? The price of holidays at www.extremeholidays.com, including tuition in snowboarding or windsurfing, begins at £495 and rises to many thousands of pounds. Insurance is vital and more costly than usual travel insurance. There is a great deal of merchandise for sale ranging from the essential (helmet, elbow and knee pads for skateboarding at £60) to the exploitative (over £200 for branded sunglasses). To bungee jump through a reputable organization costs £69.

 Through www.experience-world.co.uk it is possible to have a taste of an extreme sport during one afternoon. However, most sports require tuition, and a one-week holiday only covers basics. Skateboarding requires you to attempt a stunt, fall off, pick yourself up, and try again for as long as it takes until you succeed.

 You are most likely to think

The life that God has given me is a precious and wonderful thing, and I intend to fill every moment.

 You are least likely to think

Next time I'll just watch it on television.

Don't!

Don't let anyone persuade you to push yourself beyond limits with which you feel comfortable. And don't sue the author if you have an accident, because these sports are dangerous and you take part at your own risk!

To help you reflect

I do not run like someone running aimlessly; I do not fight like someone beating the air. No, I beat my body and make it my slave so that after I have preached to others, I myself will not be disqualified for the prize.
1 Corinthians 9.26, 27

Who shall separate us from the love of Christ? Shall trouble or hardship or persecution or famine or nakedness or danger or sword? . . . No, in all these things we are more than conquerors through him who loved us.
Romans 8.35, 37–39

The date I took part in an extreme sport

Which sport and where?

What was the most extreme moment

What I will remember between here and heaven

53 Say grace

HOW? Look at the food that is in front of you. Count the colours. Smell it and get ready to enjoy it, but hold back for a moment before taking a mouthful. Register that it is only because of the goodness of God and the work of many humans that the food is in front of you. Then tell God what you feel. If words do not come naturally, say: 'Thank you, God, for this food and for all the good things you give us. Amen.'

As saying grace becomes more natural, add variations by mentioning the name of the food, or the people with whom you are sharing the occasion. If you are by yourself, take the opportunity to thank God for other good experiences of the day. If children are with you, make the words very simple, and consider holding hands around the table so that they have a sense of a special moment in God's company. Then tuck in!

HOW EXTREME?

Here → **①** ② ③ ④ ⑤ → Heaven

What should I expect?

To state the obvious: if you are going to be thankful for your food you must be eating it in a context in which you are going to enjoy it. That is not going to happen if you are stuffing a burger down you as you walk the street, if you are more interested in the television than the taste, or if you are in a family that is eating in three separate rooms. If those are the routines into which you have fallen, there is little evidence that you are grateful for the food you are eating, and God will not be fooled. Changing those routines will be five times more extreme than saying a sentence before the first mouthful.

Be glad that God has put you in a world in which everything you need for survival exists. Then be amazed that he has chosen to do this by providing an inexhaustible variety of flavours, textures, and colours. There is no doubt whatever that this will lead to greater enjoyment of what you eat.

As it becomes habitual to pause before you eat and acknowledge that you would not be alive without God nourishing you, you will become more connected with the creator. As that happens you will also notice that you are making connections with the people through whose hands the plants or animals have passed on their way to your plate, some of whom thrive and profit as a result of it, and others who suffer injustice because of the nature of trade and find themselves in poverty, ill health or despair. You may find that this has an impact on what you pray, expanding thanks into a plea for justice and change.

Don't!

Don't try to be witty or clever. The point is not to entertain or impress the others around the table; it is to thank God.

 Nothing.

 20 seconds,
three times
a day.

 **You are
most
likely to think**

Yummy!

 **You are
least
likely to think**

This is just a meaningless
ritual done by thoughtless
people.

Who says?

You say grace before
meals. All right, but I say
grace before the concert
and the opera, and grace
before the play and
pantomime, and grace
before I open a book, and
grace before sketching,
swimming, fencing,
boxing, walking, playing,
dancing, and grace before
I dip the pen in ink.
*G.K. Chesterton, novelist,
1874–1936*

To help you reflect

*Praise the Lord, O my soul . . .
He makes grass grow for the cattle,
and plants for people to cultivate –
bringing forth food from the earth:
wine that gladdens human hearts,
oil to make their faces shine,
and bread that sustains their hearts.
Psalm 104.1, 14, 15*

*Taking the five loaves and the two fish and looking
up to heaven, [Jesus] gave thanks and broke the
loaves. Then he gave them to his disciples to set
before the people. He also divided the two fish
among them all. They all ate and were satisfied.
Mark 6.41, 42*

The date I began to say grace regularly

What I ate that day

How will I remind myself to do this without fail?

What I will remember between here and heaven

54 Investigate your Christian name

H O W ? Visit www.behindthename.com and type in your name. Having found its meaning, follow the links to discover its history, popularity over the past century, and anecdotes about people who have shared your name in life or literature. If it is possible, contact the people who gave you your name, or relatives who were alive at the time, and discover whether you were named after anyone, or the thinking that went into it. If you have changed your name, revisit the circumstances that led you to choosing it. When you have gathered all the information you can, spend some time thinking about your name, the way it has shaped your character, and whether it can reveal anything of God to you.

Do you like it? Does its meaning have any relation to events that have taken place in your life? Has the person for whom you were named had an influence on your life? Are there things about your life that have been held back by the name that you have been carrying with you? Does the fact that it is your Christian name have a spiritual significance for you?

HOW EXTREME?

Here → **❶** ② ③ ④ ⑤ → Heaven

What should I expect?

This may be very significant, or may reveal little. Some names in the Bible are given in the knowledge that they will be momentous. For example, Ahikim means 'my brother lives again', and it is easy to picture the tragic circumstances in which he received the name, and the burden it is for someone to grow up with such expectations. Other names must simply have appealed to a mother and father. Deborah sweetly means 'bee', and one can imagine the cooing and cuddling that was offered to a little Jewish girl with such a name. It may be that understanding where your name came from explains expectations that people have placed on you, opening you to rejoice in God's presence at the love that welcomed you into the world, or to seek his healing for a burden that you have had to bear.

Changes of name in the Bible mark turning points. The first leader of the Church had his name changed by Jesus from Simon ('listening') to Peter ('rock hard', which he clearly wasn't, but which gave him a vision for what he could be). Its first missionary changed his name from Saul ('an answer to prayer') to its Roman equivalent Paul ('small and unassuming', which he also wasn't, but which expressed the humility of Jesus, his role model).

Open yourself to God's showing you whether your name's meaning and background give you something to aspire to or something to rise above.

You are most likely to think

This is my Christian name, the name by which God knows me, and it is this name I will hear calling me when I am lovingly welcomed into his presence.

You are least likely to think

I wish they had called me Abishag. (It means: 'My father got up to no good', 1 Kings 1.3.)

Don't!

Don't use discoveries about your name to predict the years ahead in a superstitious way. This exercise is about reflecting on how your past has led you to this moment, and does not have any power to ruin your future.

Who says?

A signature always reveals a person's character. Sometimes it even reveals his name.
Evan Esar, North American writer, 1899–1995

To help you reflect

But now, this is what the Lord says . . .
'Fear not, for I have redeemed you;
I have summoned you by name; you are mine.'
Isaiah 43.1

[God says,] 'Can a mother forget the baby at her breast
and have no compassion on the child she has borne?
Though she may forget, I will not forget you!
See, I have engraved you on the palms of my hands.'
Isaiah 49.15, 16

The date I thought about the origin of my Christian name

This is what it means and this is how I come to have the name

How does my life compare with the meaning of my name?

What I will remember between here and heaven

55 Visit the Holy Land

HOW? Because there are parts of Israel and Palestine that are not safe (although the risk is often exaggerated) it is better to make a first visit to the Holy Land as part of a group hosted by an experienced guide. This means either joining a pilgrimage organized by a church, or booking a package tour.

Choose your company carefully. It would be possible to travel with people who contribute to the difficulty of creating a peaceful Middle East either by promoting a particular theology that excuses the injustice and violence that persist, or by choosing a route that avoids confronting the realities of life for Palestinians and Israelis who share the land that Jesus walked. Instead, an ethical travel agent such as www.responsibletravel.com offers tours that give a rounded picture by visiting places that are important to the present-day lives of Christians, Jews and Muslims, as well as historic sites.

Jerusalem has sites traditionally associated with the last week of Jesus' life and (underground, due to the passing of years) excavations of locations mentioned in the Gospels. In Palestinian territories are the places associated with Jesus' birth. Further afield, Galilee gives an enduring sense of the countryside in which Jesus began his ministry. At each significant site a church has been built, sensitive to the event that took place there. The heart of Jerusalem is sacred not only to Christians, but also to Jews as the location of the Temple, and Muslims as the site of Muhammad's ascension.

HOW EXTREME?

Here → ① ② ③ ④ ❺ → Heaven

What should I expect?

This is not a holiday, but a complete spiritual, educational and emotional experience. In Jerusalem, the tragic history of religious conflict is most sharply in focus. The historic sites are infused with a sense that we live in a world ruined by human wickedness – the very sin that led Jesus to sacrifice his life there two thousand years ago. In the open spaces of Galilee it is the message of Jesus, fresh, revolutionary and compassionate, that has most impact.

Many find that the connection between the past and the present is more vivid than they anticipated. It is impossible subsequently to read the Gospels without an increased awareness of the reality of the stories as you picture their settings. The impact of understanding the Gospel narratives in a new light, and of hearing the stories of the lives of Christians, Jews and Muslims living in the Holy Land today, means that it is vital to stop at each site long enough to pray and reflect.

How much?

The basic price for a seven-day tour is £600. Air fares add at least £250 to the cost, and you should add money for spending, food, and extra comfort if you prefer to be pampered.

Organized tours last between seven and 14 days. Flights from southern England take four hours.

Don't!

Don't mistakenly assume that when the Bible mentions Israel, the words can be applied thoughtlessly to the present-day nation, because that will skew your understanding of your visit.

You are most likely to think

Two thousand years ago, God put an intolerable strain on this land by choosing to become human here, and for 20 centuries the place has torn itself apart coming to terms with the responsibility of such a privilege.

You are least likely to think

If only I'd chosen Benidorm instead.

Who says?

Ahlan-wa-Sahlan.
An Arabic welcome, used in the Holy Land: 'When you cross our threshold, you are one of the family and you have stepped on even ground.'

To help you reflect

I rejoiced with those who said to me,
'Let us go to the house of the Lord.'
Our feet are standing in your gates, O Jerusalem . . .
Pray for the peace of Jerusalem:
'May those who love you be secure.'
Psalm 122.1, 2, 6

That which was from the beginning, which we have heard, which we have seen with our eyes, which we have looked at and our hands have touched – this we proclaim concerning the Word of life.
1 John 1.1

	The dates of my visit to the Holy Land

	Places and people that had an impact on me

	Adjectives that describe the experience

	What I will remember between here and heaven

56 Give or get bereavement counselling

HOW? Cruse Bereavement Care, through 5,000 volunteers, offers grieving people understanding of the experience they are going through, and a greater ability to cope with their loss. There are helplines (0870 167 1677, or 0808 808 1677 for young people), individual counselling, support groups and leaflets. There are also websites – www.cruse.org.uk, and www.rd4u.org.uk for children.

Cruse runs 'Loss and bereavement workshops' which introduce the issues involved in supporting people who are grieving, details of which appear on their website. However, most of its work is done through volunteers, who require no previous experience and are given training and support. Volunteers talk with bereaved people, either one-to-one, as part of a group, or by telephone. Click 'Volunteering' at the top of the website homepage in order to make contact, or write to Cruse Bereavement Care, 126 Sheen Road, Richmond, TW9 1UR. Scotland has an independent Cruse organization at Riverview House, Friarton Road, Perth, PH2 8DF.

Of the many books written to help Christian people find a path through their bereavement, *A Grief Observed*, C.S. Lewis's account of his experience after the death of his wife, remains outstanding.

HOW EXTREME?

Here → ① ② ③ ④ ❺ → Heaven

What should I expect?

Grieving people go (at different paces and in cycles) through phases of shock and denial, isolation, anger, bargaining, depression, acceptance and hope. This is a God-given process that enables people to be fully human in the way they respond to death, and there are no short cuts, even for people with a profound belief in heaven. The function of counselling is to help people free themselves from being permanently in slavery to the loss they have suffered, to readjust to the environment without the deceased person in it, and to create a context in which new relationships can form.

A sensitive Christian can have a special ministry in helping a grieving person deal with their loss, because his or her faith can unlock permission for the person who has been bereaved to talk about spiritual concerns, be they doubt, anger with God, or a search for assurance about what lies beyond death. As a representative of a community of faith in which the hope of resurrection is alive, a Christian can help a mourner begin to make sense of their loss. However, bereaved people are extremely vulnerable, and training is needed in order to approach counselling in a way that reconciles people to a community of life, and does not unwittingly manipulate them into a religious response.

There is no charge for volunteers to train through Cruse, or for people to make use of their services. However, they rely almost completely on charity donations. 'Loss and bereavement workshops' for professionals cost £141. *A Grief Observed* (Faber Paperbacks) costs £6.99.

A bereavement counselling session usually lasts 50 minutes. The person who has been bereaved and the counsellor decide how many times to meet at the end of their first session. However, there is no rule about how long it takes to recover from loss, and grief dictates its own pace.

You are most likely to think

To be allowed to share someone's grief is to be invited into the part of their life that is most precious and spiritually alive.

Don't!

Don't ever tell someone who has been bereaved what they ought to think or feel.

You are least likely to think

Cheer up!

Who says?

Be not hasty to offer advice to those who are bowed down with a weight of trouble. There is a sacredness in grief which demands our reverence; the very habitation of a mourner must be approached with awe.
Charles Simeon, clergyman, 1759–1836

To help you reflect

[Jesus said,] 'Blessed are those who mourn, for they will be comforted.'
Matthew 5.4

Brothers and sisters, we do not want you to be ignorant about those who fall asleep, or to grieve like the rest, who have no hope. We believe that Jesus died and rose again and so we believe that God will bring with Jesus those who have fallen asleep in him.
1 Thessalonians 4.13, 14

The date I received or gave bereavement counselling

What were the circumstances?

Some of the emotions I was aware of

What I will remember between here and heaven

57 Listen to a choral masterpiece

HOW? Find details of concerts in newspapers or from the brochures of concert halls. You can identify choral concerts because the name of the choir performing will be listed. Venues include the Royal Albert Hall, London, where BBC Promenade concerts (Proms) are performed from July to September, and the Usher Hall, one of the venues for the Edinburgh Festival during August. Most cathedrals have weekly services in which an outstanding choir sings church music, and times are published on their websites.

Readily enjoyable works include *Spem in alium* (by the 16th-century composer Thomas Tallis – an undulating sea of harmonies whose words mean, 'I have never put my hope in anyone but you, God'), *Messiah* (by George Handel, an 18th-century oratorio about the significance of Jesus), or *Mass in B minor* (by Johann Sebastian Bach, a setting of the Latin words used in a communion service). Contemporary masterpieces include *Song for Athene* (by John Tavener, interweaving words from a funeral service with others from Shakespeare's *Hamlet*, 'Flights of angels sing thee to thy rest').

HOW EXTREME?

Here → ① **❷** ③ ④ ⑤ → Heaven

What should I expect?

Most European choral masterpieces are settings of Christian texts. As the music proceeds, try to recognize the moods and make connections with experiences in the Christian life – mystery, sadness, yearning, and occasionally triumphant joy. If the piece is performed well you will glimpse these even without knowing the meaning of the words.

A booklet in which an expert puts the composition in context is usually available, but listening to a choral masterpiece requires no previous knowledge. Simply let the music affect you – awakening feelings, activating memories, touching your heart. Although there is an etiquette of concert-going (for instance, applauding when the piece is finished, not between each song), it can easily be learnt by copying others.

If you are listening to live classical music for the first time, notice different speeds and instrument sounds, loudness and softness, and the way the high voices of the choir (female sopranos or boy trebles) contrast with the deep ones (basses). Allow visual images of the life of Jesus to suggest themselves, or let the atmosphere at different points bring truths from the Bible to mind. As the singers, doing something difficult with great skill, create a united sound, bring to mind God's desire to draw all humankind together in harmony with him.

Ticket prices range from £5 to stand at the Proms to £40 for the best seats at the Edinburgh Festival. On a first visit, choose a lower priced ticket (£10–£15) allowing you to hear well but view from a distance. Cathedral services are usually free.

Spem in alium lasts 11 minutes and *Song for Athene* 7 minutes. Both are performed as part of a longer programme of music. *Messiah* lasts 140 minutes and *Mass in B minor* 110 minutes.

Who says?

The aim and final end of all music should be none other than the glory of God and the refreshment of the soul.
Johann Sebastian Bach, composer, 1685–1750

You are most likely to think

These voices, rising and falling in harmony, have set my mind on heaven.

You are least likely to think

Come back Sex Pistols, all is forgiven!

Don't!

Don't sing along, even if you recognize the tune.

To help you reflect

In a loud voice [the angels] sang: 'Worthy is the Lamb, who was slain, to receive power and wealth and wisdom and strength and honour and glory and praise!' Then I heard every creature in heaven and on earth and under the earth and on the sea, and all that is in them, singing: 'To him who sits on the throne and to the Lamb be praise and honour and glory and power, for ever and ever!'
Revelation 5.12, 13

Sing joyfully to the Lord, you righteous;
it is fitting for the upright to praise him.
Praise the Lord with the harp;
make music to him on the ten-stringed lyre.
Sing to him a new song;
play skilfully, and shout for joy.
Psalm 33.1–3

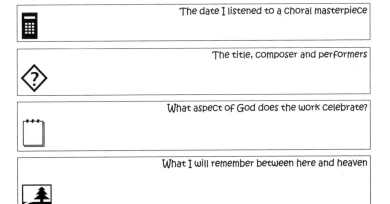

The date I listened to a choral masterpiece

The title, composer and performers

What aspect of God does the work celebrate?

What I will remember between here and heaven

58 Sell your possessions at a car boot sale

HOW? This is a way of unburdening yourself of old clothes, toys, furniture and jewellery while making money for a good cause or to fund a treat. About 300 upcoming sales are listed at www.carbootjunction.com, and you can link from there to lists of smaller, local sales.

You do not need to book a pitch (although regulars are usually given early entry and get the best positions). You should, however, arrive over an hour before the public is admitted. If you do not have a car, smaller sales have a walk-in service, allowing you to set up a folding table with goods.

You will need large boxes to carry your goods in, plastic bags for your sales, about £30 in coins, and a bumbag to keep the change safe and handy. Present your stock as well as you can, taking a rail if you have clothes to sell, and include a box of smaller items because people love rooting through them for a bargain.

HOW EXTREME?

Here → ① ❷ ③ ④ ⑤ → Heaven

What should I expect?

When Jesus told his followers to sell their possessions and give the money to the poor he cannot have imagined car boot sales. However, he did realize that the clutter which gathers around you distracts you from following him. His first followers sold anything they did not need (and much that they did) and with it created a fund that strengthened vulnerable people. This was so impressive to outsiders that they joined the church in large numbers.

Allow the question of what you do with your profit to give you pleasure. Devise a plan to do good with it. Anticipate that someone (a friend, someone in need, or a stranger who will benefit through a charity) will have their life improved in a way that is quite unexpected. Then you will enjoy the selling, crowds will enjoy the buying, others will enjoy the profit. How could it be better!

 Who says?

I am still looking for the modern day equivalents of those Quakers who ran successful businesses, made money because they offered honest products and treated their people decently, worked hard, spent honestly, saved honestly, gave honest value for money, put more back than they took out, and told no lies.
Anita Roddick, founder of The Body Shop cosmetic retail chain

How much?

Expect to pay £9 to £11 for a pitch. However, anticipate going home in profit. As a general rule, something brand new sells for about one-fifth of its original price, and about one-tenth if it looks worn but well looked after. Have a vague pricing structure in mind – say 20p for a book, £1 for a piece of costume jewellery, £5 for a good item of clothing. However, be ready to barter because no one will give you the amount you first quote.

Sales last for 4–6 hours, with the gates opening to sellers an hour early (but queues form before popular sales, and you should be braced for an early start).

 You are most likely to think

My life is better without this clutter, so I will do something worthwhile with the profit.

 You are least likely to think

I wish I hadn't parted with that lava lamp.

Don't!

Don't hoodwink a customer, since you are subject to trading standards law even if you only do this once in a lifetime, and must give a refund if you describe goods inaccurately.

To help you reflect

All the believers were together and had everything in common. Selling their possessions and goods, they gave to anyone as he had need. Every day they continued to meet together in the temple courts. They broke bread in their homes and ate together with glad and sincere hearts, praising God and enjoying the favour of all the people. And the Lord added to their number daily those who were being saved.
Acts 2.44–47

Honest scales and balances are from the Lord; all the weights in the bag are of his making.
Proverbs 16.11

The date I sold my possessions at a car boot sale

My profit at the end of the day

My best sales

What I will remember between here and heaven

59 Have an alternative Christmas

HOW? Many projects for vulnerable people need extra volunteers at Christmas because the usual lines of support close for the holiday season. In particular, projects for homeless people offer shelter, food and companionship during the coldest nights of the year. In London, Crisis Open Christmas is the largest such project, and there are similar schemes in other cities. They require specialist volunteers (such as qualified kitchen staff, hairdressers, drivers and journalists), and those who can offer general help with serving meals and befriending guests.

Other schemes offer hospitality to asylum seekers, and elderly or lonely people. To find a local project, type 'Christmas' into the search engine at www.timebank.org.uk, www.salvationarmy.org.uk, or www.crisis.org.uk. Make contact with the organization requesting volunteers, and find out whether you can match its needs with your availability. They will provide forms, and guide you through the application process.

HOW EXTREME?

Here → ① ② ③ ❹ ⑤ → Heaven

What should I expect?

Because Christmas can be a time of indulgence, it is natural that Christians are eager to give it a practical meaning by serving vulnerable people. Because Christmas is a celebration of the joys of indoors, it is appropriate that their thoughts turn particularly to those who are homeless. And because Christmas recognizes that God has been born among us, spending the holiday alongside those who need to experience his love and care is an obvious alternative to focusing on food and entertainment.

Some people volunteer their time in the service of others at Christmas expecting to feel richly fulfilled, but end up exhausted and dirty rather than elated. You ought to bear in mind, when you choose a project, that your objective is not primarily your own reward, but the pleasure that others will have. That would reflect Jesus' own actions, emptying himself of every aspect of his heavenly existence in order to be born in poverty, completely vulnerable, and without any kind of guarantee that the sacrifice would be acknowledged or welcomed by those he came to save. Giving without expecting anything in return is entirely true to the spirit of the Christian Christmas. Paradoxically, those who volunteer with that attitude are those who are most likely to find the experience thoroughly worthwhile.

Don't!

Don't deprive someone whom you know of the time they genuinely need to share with you because of your determination to be generous to strangers.

It is rare for Christmas projects to reimburse expenses, but they take the comfort of their volunteers seriously and ensure that those travelling late at night are not at risk. Most provide meals during shifts.

Crisis Open Christmas divides the day into shifts of about eight hours, and asks volunteers to commit to at least two and at most eight between Christmas Eve and New Year's Day. This is typical, but every project is different. Many have training days in early December.

You are most likely to think

If Jesus was on earth now, this is how he would have spent today.

You are least likely to think

Drat! I missed the *Eastenders* Christmas special!

Who says?

Use your discernment and choose the course that takes you farthest away from the deadening activities of the stifling world, and brings you close to God. Direct your footsteps toward Bethlehem like the blessed Magi, your fellow companions, until you reach the appointed place of that blessed star.
Babai, leader of the church in Assyria, 551–628

To help you reflect

The grace of God that brings salvation has appeared to all people. It teaches us to say 'No' to ungodliness and worldly passions, and to live self-controlled, upright and godly lives in this present age, while we wait for the blessed hope.
Titus 2.11–13

Your attitude should be the same as that of Christ Jesus who, being in very nature God, did not consider equality with God something to be grasped, but made himself nothing, taking the very nature of a servant, being made in human likeness.
Philippians 2.5–7

The date I spent Christmas in an alternative way

What I did and where

How did it improve someone else's life?

What I will remember between here and heaven

60 Analyse yourself with Myers-Briggs

HOW? Two North American psychologists, Katharine Briggs and her daughter Isabel Myers, devised a test in 1940 that helps people understand why their personality leads them to prefer working, praying and relating to others in a particular way. Influenced by Carl Jung's theories, the test involves 93 questions that ask you to choose between alternatives such as, 'Are you more interested in starting projects or finishing projects?' The answers, once analysed, position you on scales according to your preferences. These divide people into 16 distinct personality types.

The test lends itself to exploring your spirituality, as well as your God-given personality, so many certified Myers-Briggs analysts are also Christians. Courses are widely available, and most retreat centres (listed at www.retreats.org.uk) run them regularly or may be able to help you find one. *Knowing Me, Knowing God: Exploring Your Spirituality with Myers-Briggs*, by Malcolm Goldsmith (Triangle), is a book that allows you to take the test by yourself. It can also be taken online at www.discoveryourpersonality.com/MBTI.html, where the service includes a written report and a telephone consultation.

HOW EXTREME?

Here → **❶** ② ③ ④ ⑤ → Heaven

What should I expect?

The scales show your preference between Extrovert and Introvert (E/I – preferring to focus on the external world of objects and people, or the inner world of ideas and feelings); Sensing or Intuition (S/N – perceiving the world directly through the five senses, or processing the information through the unconscious to produce intuitive responses); Thinking or Feeling (T/F – making decisions in rational 'true or false', or individualized 'better or worse' ways); and Judging or Perceiving (J/P – preferring a step by step approach with rules that lead to a conclusion, or an approach that leaves options open and relies on subjective judgements). Together they create a four-letter personality type (for instance, ESTJ).

Knowing your personality helps you understand yourself, but it is also important for understanding others. What you once saw as inexplicably irritating attitudes emerge as strengths that can complement your own weaknesses in a team or congregation. It can lift guilt about not finding it easy to pray in a particular way and open possibilities for drawing close to God that are better suited to the way he created you.

Who says?

Who we are is how we pray.
Charles Keating, North American devotional writer

A residential Myers-Briggs course at Wychcroft, Bletchingly, Surrey costs £130, including overnight accommodation, which is a typical price. *Knowing Me, Knowing God* costs £4.99. To take the test online costs £40. A free online test, which is intriguing but does not give you the means of applying the information to your life, can be found at www. personalitytypes. net/types.

The most valuable courses, which include space for reflection and discussion, are spread over two days. Others squeeze the process into one day. Answering the questions of the test itself takes about half an hour.

You are most likely to think

I now understand that people who disagree with me about how to worship, learn and serve God are not wrong, just different.

You are least likely to think

Of course, the way I do it is better.

Don't!

Don't assume that because you have a particular personality you cannot operate in any other way. Your type shows why you like certain things, not that you are incapable of doing others (just as left-handed people don't give up using their right hand). For instance, temperamentally Sensing people are capable of sitting through a sermon, although there are better ways for them to learn about God.

To help you reflect

There are different kinds of gifts, but the same Spirit. There are different kinds of service, but the same Lord. There are different kinds of working, but the same God works all of them in everyone. Now to each one the manifestation of the Spirit is given for the common good.
1 Corinthians 12.4–7

Those who get wisdom love their own souls; those who cherish understanding prosper . . . A person's wisdom yields patience; it is to one's glory to overlook an offence.
Proverbs 19.8, 11

The date I took a Myers-Briggs test

My personality type

Something I understood about myself for the first time

What I will remember between here and heaven

61 Give to the world's poorest people

HOW? Consider which of the many charities that fund work in the developing world best matches your ideas. A large organization that benefits many people, or a small one that funds a few specific projects? A Christian charity that includes prayer in its methodology, or a secular one that brings together generous people of all faiths and none? An organization that campaigns to change the root causes of poverty, or one that responds to emergencies with aid? Visit www.charitychoice.co.uk and click on the 'Overseas aid' segment of the 'Charity category search'. Follow the links to the websites listed, or telephone and ask for information to be sent in the post. After comparing and choosing, fill in a direct debit form to make a monthly payment. If you pay income tax and tick the relevant box, the government will add 28 per cent to the value of your gift by allowing the charity to reclaim the tax.

HOW EXTREME?

Here → ① ❷ ③ ④ ⑤ → Heaven

What should I expect?

From the very beginning of God's dealings with his people, practical action for the poor has been singled out as the clearest evidence of a life lived as God intends. The Old Testament laws made provision for widows, orphans and refugees unable to fend for themselves. It was not a handout, but a system that allowed poor people the dignity of working their own way out of poverty. Jesus, announcing the priorities of his mission, quoted a passage from Isaiah about bringing good news to the poor and relieving the plight of those who were suffering. And the letters of the New Testament, written during a time of famine, give explicit instructions to Christians who had more than enough to give money to those in need.

Each subsequent generation of Christians – the desert fathers, the Franciscans, the Victorian reformers, present-day campaigners – has made the pursuit of justice for those who have been made poor by the luxury of others central to the expression of their faith. So you should feel satisfied to be part of a centuries-old desire to reflect the compassion and justice that is in God's own nature.

Don't!

Don't make the arrangement through a person who stops you in the street. The agency organizing this will charge the charity anything up to the first year's worth of your donation. To maximize the percentage of your money that goes to the developing world, make direct contact with a charity.

How much?

Research by charities shows that the amount most people are inclined to give on a regular basis is £2 per month. (This is why letters from charities often suggest this amount as a donation that would have a worthwhile impact on a poor community.) Measure your generosity against that.

15 minutes to set up a direct debit, which will subsequently ensure payments are made without any further investment of time.

You are most likely to think

Giving money is just a start. Now I need to pressurize politicians to change the circumstances that trap people in poverty.

You are least likely to think

What will they give me in return?

Who says?

The question to be asked is not, 'What should we give to the poor?' but, 'When will we stop taking from the poor?' The poor are not our problem; we are their problem.
Jim Wallis, founder of the Sojourners Community in Washington, USA

To help you reflect

To despise the poor is to sin, but blessed are those who are kind to the needy.
Proverbs 14.21

[Jesus said:] 'Do not be afraid, little flock, for your Father has been pleased to give you the kingdom. Sell your possessions and give to the poor. Provide purses for yourselves that will not wear out, a treasure in heaven that will not be exhausted, where no thief comes near and no moth destroys. For where your treasure is, there your heart will be also.'
Luke 12.32–34

The date I started a regular payment to the world's poorest people

How much and to whom?

Which poor country or group of people inspired me to give?

What I will remember between here and heaven

123

62 Say the Jesus prayer

HOW? The Jesus prayer dates back to the 5th century and is important in Orthodox traditions of Christianity. It involves repeating a short prayer to Jesus over and over again. The words often used are: 'Lord Jesus Christ, Son of God, have mercy on me, the sinner' (words originally spoken by Bartimaeus to Jesus).

First, the words are spoken consciously and you concentrate on their meaning. Then the repetition allows you to enter a meditative state of prayer, in which you draw close to God in a way that is beyond words. Finally the words give way into a silence in which you and God are at rest in each other's company – what the Bible describes as 'prayer without ceasing'.

In Eastern Europe a rope of knots (chokti) is used to focus your mind. You hold the first knot between your fingers, say the prayer, then move to the next knot each time you repeat it. This is a less intrusive method than a clock of measuring how long you are at prayer.

HOW EXTREME?

Here → ① ❷ ③ ④ ⑤ → Heaven

What should I expect?

The Jesus prayer is a way to allow adoration and repentance to descend from your mind to your heart, leaving you to gaze on God. There are no clever words said to impress other people. But it is far from meaningless, since it leads you into the same kind of humility that Jesus valued when he told a parable about a tax collector who was so conscious of his need of God that he was reduced to whispering these words repeatedly. You may find yourself drawn into an inner peace in which prayer has ceased to be something you do, and become something you are. In that state, God is able to make you deeply aware of the love he has for you, and of the absolute need you have for him as your saviour. It is as if God would gladly have given himself for you if you alone were the only needy human in the world.

How much?

Nothing.

 15 minutes or more, until words give way to loving silence. Orthodox monks make this part of a long night of prayer, repeating it hundreds of times.

Don't!

Don't lose heart if you are distracted. Ease yourself back to the prayer knowing that, although your mind wandered away, Jesus did not.

Who says?

When I prayed with all my heart, everything around me seemed delightful and marvellous. The trees, the grass, the birds, the air, the light seemed to be telling me that they exist for the sake of humankind, that they witness to the love of God for humans, that all things pray to God and sing his praise . . . I did not walk along as before, filled with care. The invocation of the name of Jesus gladdened my way. Everybody was kind to me. If anyone harmed me I had only to think, 'How sweet is the Jesus Prayer,' and the injury and the anger alike passed away.
The Way of a Pilgrim, an anonymous book of Orthodox spirituality, 19th century

You are most likely to think

I belong to my Lord and my Lord belongs to me. This is the most important thing in life.

You are least likely to think

I hope I have impressed other people by saying this.

To help you reflect

A blind man, Bartimaeus . . . was sitting by the roadside begging. When he heard that it was Jesus of Nazareth, he began to shout, 'Jesus, Son of David, have mercy on me!' Many rebuked him and told him to be quiet, but he shouted all the more, 'Son of David, have mercy on me!' . . . 'What do you want me to do for you?' Jesus asked him. The blind man said, 'Rabbi, I want to see.' 'Go,' said Jesus, 'your faith has healed you.' Immediately he received his sight and followed Jesus along the road.
Mark 10.46–52

Through Jesus, therefore, let us continually offer to God a sacrifice of praise – the fruit of lips that confess his name.
Hebrews 13.15

	The date I said the Jesus prayer

	For how long?

	My feelings before, during and after

	What I will remember between here and heaven

125

63 Clear out the cupboards

HOW? Begin by hardening your heart. Then be pitiless! Get four boxes and label them: 'Put away', 'Give away', 'Store away' and 'Throw away'. Start in the kitchen and work one cupboard at a time. Empty its contents completely, and clean inside. Divide everything that was in it into one of the four boxes.

Pick up the items one at a time. If it is food that has passed its sell-by date, throw it away immediately. If you have never used it, make a snap decision about whether to throw it away or give it away, but resist all temptation to put it back. If you haven't used it in the last year, do the same. Particular ruthlessness is needed with equipment that was expensive, but you never use (for example, the ten-year-old toasted sandwich maker in a greasy corner). The exceptions are things that are vital once a year, at Christmas for instance, which could be stored in a place where they are not in the way. When you are left with items that you will certainly use, put them back in a logical order, with those you use daily easily accessible, and those you use less often on higher shelves.

Move on from the kitchen to other storage cupboards and drawers. Pay special attention to surfaces on which you tend to put things down haphazardly. Move on to tidy your CDs and DVDs (being unsentimental about things you no longer have the technology to play). If you have a garage or a loft, keep going!

HOW EXTREME?

Here → ① ❷ ③ ④ ⑤ → Heaven

What should I expect?

This will relieve you of wasted time, anxiety and possibly money. Keys and remote controls will be found in an instant. Bills will no longer accumulate interest because you lose them under a heap of paper. But rumours of the Declutter Pixie, who comes during the night and does this for you, are not true. He has eloped with the Tooth Fairy. It's down to you!

However, doing this can also have a spiritual significance. As you find yourself letting go of things that have collected dust, you will find your attitude changing too. It is a kind of repentance, turning your back on what is unnecessary. Things that distract your attention from the way that God has laid out before you will disappear, people will become more important than objects, and you will become clearer about your priorities. You may even have a physical sensation of being cleansed, as though wrongdoing has been forgiven. When what is superfluous has gone from the house, and you look around to see what is left, you will find yourself looking at people you love, and you will sense God.

Nothing.

How much?

Make an early start, allow four hours, then have a celebratory lunch.

 You are least likely to think

Oh how I wish I had kept that novelty jelly mould!

 You are most likely to think

I'm going to keep it this way.

Don't!

Don't throw away anything that speaks of someone's love for you, even if that breaks all the rules you have decided on.

Who says?

If there is something you own that you can't give away, you don't own it – it owns you.
Albert Schweitzer, doctor and missionary to Africa, 1875–1965

To help you reflect

Whatever was to my profit I now consider loss for the sake of Christ. What is more, I consider everything a loss compared to the surpassing greatness of knowing Christ Jesus my Lord, for whose sake I have lost all things. I consider them rubbish, that I may gain Christ and be found in him.
Philippians 3.7–9

Do not store up for yourselves treasures on earth, where moth and rust destroy, and where thieves break in and steal. But store up for yourselves treasures in heaven, where moth and rust do not destroy, and where thieves do not break in and steal. For where your treasure is, there your heart will be also.
Matthew 6.19–21

The date I cleared out the cupboards

I am glad to be rid of these

I had forgotten I own these

What I will remember between here and heaven

127

64 Ride a roller coaster

HOW? Roller coasters vary in intensity from the charming and breezy Scenic Railway in Margate's Dreamland (dating from 1920, its elegant wooden construction now a listed building) to the heart-stopping Rita at Staffordshire's Alton Towers (which reaches 100 miles per hour from a standstill within 2½ seconds). Links to the sites of the world's major roller coasters can be found at the website of the Roller Coaster Club of Great Britain (www.rccgb.co.uk).

Tickets for most roller coasters can only be obtained as part of a day pass to a theme park containing many attractions. During school holidays, queues develop at the most popular rides, and it is wise to be at the park when it opens and go straight to the roller coaster that you want to ride. Careful attention is paid to safety in theme parks. Riders are very secure inside the carriage, but are responsible for ensuring that they do not lose hats, cash or belongings as the train turns at great speed.

HOW EXTREME?

Here → ① ② ③ ❹ ⑤ → Heaven

What should I expect?

Riding a roller coaster is basically a visceral experience, in which your body goes through extreme physical sensations. Those who enjoy roller coasters talk in particular about the excitement of surrendering to an experience that generates fear, but promises safety. The body has no control over what is happening to it, and can feel weightless and intensely heavy within seconds of each other. Those who hate roller coasters do so for the very same reasons.

To describe the experience as spiritual may be an exaggeration. However, a ride on a roller coaster makes you acutely aware of the body in which God has placed you, with its potential and limitations. Because your senses become first numb, and then intensely conscious of every feeling, sight and sound, it is possible to become aware both of your connection to the earth on which all humans live, and also the difference between being alive and being clay. People who yelp with joy as they walk away from the ride may be praising God for their existence without even realizing it.

How much?

💰 The standard entrance fee for an adult to a theme park is in the region of £28, but there are many reductions available for young people, groups, advance bookings and visits out of season. Add the cost of travel and food (after the roller coaster, not before).

🕐 Travel, anticipation, plucking up courage, queuing . . . and then about two minutes.

128

Don't!

Don't risk your health if you know you have a medical condition that makes it unwise for your body to be put under strain. And don't get talked into doing something you are not confident about, because they won't stop the train for you once it has started.

 Who says?

I owned the world that hour as I rode over it. Free of the earth, free of the mountains, free of the clouds, but how inseparably I was bound to them . . . A certain amount of danger is essential to the quality of life . . . God made life simple. It is man who complicated it.
Charles Lindbergh, aviator, 1902–1974

 You are most likely to think

Aaaaaeea-eeoyee-ooo-iyaiyaiya-nthnthnth-errrrr-aaaaooa.

 You are least likely to think

Now, let me analyse this intellectually!

To help you reflect

*They mounted up to the heavens and went down
    to the depths;
in their peril their courage melted away.
They reeled and staggered like drunkards;
they were at their wits' end.
Then they cried out to the Lord in their trouble,
and he brought them out of their distress.
He stilled the storm to a whisper;
the waves of the sea were hushed.
They were glad when it grew calm,
and he guided them to their desired haven.
Let them give thanks to the Lord for his unfailing
    love
and his wonderful deeds for human beings.*
Psalm 107.26–31

I commend the enjoyment of life, because nothing is better for people under the sun than to eat and drink and be glad. Then joy will accompany them in their work all the days of the life God has given them.
Ecclesiastes 8.15

The date I rode a roller coaster

Where was it?

Adjectives that describe the experience

What I will remember between here and heaven

65 Find your first home

HOW? This may be easy (you may, for instance, still live in the house where you were born) or involve research and travel. If you know where you were born, visit by train, plane or car. Walk around the area, trying to work out what remains from the date you were born, and what has been knocked down or redeveloped. Crouch, so that you can see the place from the perspective you had as a child. Introduce yourself to minimize the suspicion caused by someone loitering outside a house or taking photographs. If you do not know where you lived in your earliest days, begin by asking relatives. If that is not possible, find out how to get a copy of your birth certificate or information about your adoption at www.familyrecords.gov.uk.

HOW EXTREME?

Here → ① ❷ ③ ④ ⑤ → Heaven

What should I expect?

Your experience will vary depending on whether you look back on your early years as joyful or miserable. Unless you left your birthplace at a very young age, the sights (and, more potently, the smells) will bring back recollections that would otherwise be buried. Looking at the setting to which your mother took you after your birth may help you understand the circumstances in which things happened when you were young, or may leave you with further questions that can only be answered by conversation with relatives.

As happy memories return, offer them to God, one by one, with thanksgiving. As unhappy memories arise, tell God about the healing that you need so that you will no longer be held back or trapped by the feelings they generate. Prepare to be disappointed by change or realization that your assumptions have been over-romantic – offer that to God as well. Whatever emotions arise, try to allow what you can see at your first home to help you understand more about why those who nurtured you in your infancy took the decisions they did.

How much?

The price of travel to and from the location. A copy of your birth certificate from the Family Records Office costs from £7, depending on how quickly you want it and how complicated the search is.

Too varied to predict, depending on how much research and travel is required.

Don't!

Don't knock on the door of your first home and assume that the current occupant will spontaneously welcome a stranger in. If you wish to make contact, write in advance, prove your identity, treat the owner's caution with understanding, and be prepared to accept no for an answer.

 ## Who says?

I remember, I remember,
The house where I was born,
The little window where the sun
Came peeping in at morn . . .
I remember, I remember,
The fir trees dark and high;
I used to think their slender tops
Were close against the sky:
It was a childish ignorance,
But now 'tis little joy
To know I'm farther off from heav'n
Than when I was a boy.
Thomas Hood, poet,
1799–1845

 ## You are most likely to think

I have not travelled from this place to where I live today by a series of random accidents. God has journeyed with me and there has been a purpose to every turn of the route.

 ## You are least likely to think

It's bigger than I expected.

To help you reflect

Listen to me, you who pursue righteousness
and who seek the Lord:
Look to the rock from which you were cut
and to the quarry from which you were hewn . . .
The Lord will surely comfort Zion
and will look with compassion on all her ruins . . .
Joy and gladness will be found in her,
thanksgiving and the sound of singing.
Isaiah 51.1–3

You created my inmost being;
you knit me together in my mother's womb.
I praise you because I am fearfully and
wonderfully made;
your works are wonderful, I know that full well.
My frame was not hidden from you when I was
made in the secret place.
Psalm 139.13–15

	The date I revisited the place of my birth

	Where is it?

	The difference between my expectations and the reality

	What I will remember between here and heaven

66 Buy nothing for a day

HOW? Spend 24 hours living more simply, and without parting with cash, cheques or credit cards. This includes money spent on food, travel, entertainment, bills and so on. For some regular purchases this will involve forgoing non-essentials (for instance, newspapers or snacks). For others, some advance planning will be involved. Work out how necessary travel can be paid for in advance, or walk. Use up food you have in the house instead of buying more. Pay bills in advance or the day after. Make presents for people instead of buying them. Think imaginatively about what could be borrowed or shared with friends. (There is no need to be pedantic about direct debits or subscriptions. This is a statement of intent, not a trial by ordeal.)

A national 'Buy Nothing Day' is promoted in the UK on the last Saturday in November (www.buynothingday.co.uk).

HOW EXTREME?

Here → ① ② ❸ ④ ⑤ → Heaven

What should I expect?

It is possible to treat a day without shopping as either a personal experiment or a public statement. Its purpose is not really to save money, but to increase your awareness of where your money goes. For example, to pay a bill the day before or the day after will not change the price, but will focus your mind more clearly on how much things cost, and whether they are really necessary.

Every time you register that you have had to change your routine in order to avoid spending money, bring to mind some of the issues involved in being a consumer. Twenty per cent of the world's population consumes 80 per cent of the resources God has placed on the earth, causing an unfair division of the world's wealth and a disproportionate level of environmental damage.

Lasting for a day without buying anything is more challenging that it appears. One person's stance will not, of course, have any impact at all on retailers, and the country will not grind to a halt. However, you may end the day feeling that you have more control over your life than usual. And it may lead you to make a decision to consume less, recycle more, and to pressurize corporations to do their business in a cleaner and fairer way.

Don't!

Don't risk your health or happiness. Check the day before that you have first aid, and that you are not going to offend friends.

Absolutely and gloriously nothing.

No time at all, but fill the time with something wonderful instead.

You are most likely to think

Can I do without it? Could I borrow one? Can I clean or repair it myself, rather than pay for it to be done? How will I dispose of it when I have finished with it? What are the environmental consequences of using it? Is there anything I already own that I could substitute?

You are least likely to think

I can't afford to do that again.

Who says?

God wants to give us something, but he cannot, because our hands are full. There's nowhere for him to put it.
Augustine, bishop of Hippo, 354–430

To help you reflect

[Jesus said,] 'Do not worry, saying, "What shall we eat?" or "What shall we drink?" or "What shall we wear?" For the pagans run after all these things, and your heavenly Father knows that you need them. But seek first his kingdom and his righteousness, and all these things will be given to you as well. Therefore do not worry about tomorrow, for tomorrow will worry about itself. Each day has enough trouble of its own.'
Matthew 6.31–34

[Jesus] said to them, 'Watch out! Be on your guard against all kinds of greed; life does not consist in the abundance of possessions.'
Luke 12.15

The date I went without buying anything

What difference did it make to the routines of my day?

What was the most awkward moment?

What I will remember between here and heaven

67 Visit an ancient Christian site

HOW? A substantial list of ancient religious sites (mostly Christian, but some pre-Christian) can be found at www.sacredsites.com. Click 'Europe' at the top of the screen, and scroll down to 'England (Map of England's sacred places)' to identify sites in England, Scotland and Wales, and 'Ireland (Map of Ireland's sacred places)' for Northern Ireland and the Republic. Choose a place that intrigues you and type its name into a search engine to find historical information and advice about how to travel there. For more detail, refer to *The Traveller's Guide to Sacred Ireland* (Cary Meehan, Gothic Image) and *Sacred Britain* (Martin Palmer and Nigel Palmer, Piatkus).

Among many others you might choose the spartan monastery clinging to the bare rocks of the Skellig Islands, off County Kerry, Ireland, whose 'beehive' stone cells have stood since 588. Or the ruins of Whithorn Priory, Galloway, where Ninian founded the first large Christian community in Scotland in 397. Or St Non's Well in Pembrokeshire, where in 512 Non gave birth to David, the great spiritual leader of Wales and later its patron saint. Or St Peter's Chapel, Bradwell, Essex, where after years of neglect when it was used as a cattle shed, England's first cathedral has been restored to the state in which it was consecrated by Cedd in 654.

HOW EXTREME?

Here → ① ② ❸ ④ ⑤ → Heaven

What should I expect?

The earliest Christian communities in Britain and Ireland were attracted to off-shore islands and the edges of the land. There they could both retreat to be self-contained communities set apart for God, and also advance, using their home as a base from which to take the good news of Jesus from the fringes to the mainstream. Their isolation makes ancient Christian sites places of quiet serenity, and in the peace it is possible to experience a powerful sense of the Spirit of God making you one with those who have shared your faith in centuries long gone. The ruins are sometimes just unexceptional stones, but they mark indelibly the presence of faith. You will realize that time has worn very thin the space between the sacred and the everyday.

Picture the Christians who first worshipped God in these places, and recall their prayers that a nation which knew nothing of Jesus would be transformed by encountering him. Those prayers were answered in a way that exceeded anything they imagined. Then recognize that, in some ways, today's Christians worship in the same small numbers on the edges of society, and let your hopes soar.

How much?

The Traveller's Guide to Sacred Ireland costs £18.95, and Sacred Britain £16.50. The cost of travel to pilgrimage sites varies, but some can be expensive to reach because of their remoteness. The crossing to the Skellig Islands costs 35 euros (about £23). Admission to Whithorn Priory is £3, but there is no charge to visit St Peter's Chapel or St Non's Well.

Visits to ancient Christian sites require several hours in order to understand their history and to sense the power of succeeding generations praying in that place.

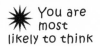 **You are most likely to think**

My brothers and sisters have kept the faith alive among these stones for hundreds of years, and I want to be as faithful as them in my generation.

Don't!

Don't leave without adding to the prayers for the nation that have been said there for countless generations.

 You are least likely to think

Everything was easier for the Christians of previous centuries.

 Who says?

Let your feet follow your heart until you find your place of resurrection.
Anonymous, possibly Columbanus, Irish monk and missionary, 540–615

To help you reflect

This is what the Lord says: 'Stand at the crossroads and look; ask for the ancient paths, ask where the good way is, and walk in it, and you will find rest for your souls.'
Jeremiah 6.16

Listen to me, you who pursue righteousness and who seek the Lord: Look to the rock from which you were cut and to the quarry from which you were hewn.
Isaiah 51.1

The date I visited an ancient Christian site

Where? And what is there to see?

The impact it had on me

What I will remember between here and heaven

68 Read religious poetry

HOW? Buy or borrow an anthology such as *The Lion Book of Christian Poetry* (edited by Mary Batchelor) or *The New Oxford Book of Religious Verse* (edited by Davie Donald). Do not attempt to read it from beginning to end, but drift around the book, allowing poems to catch your attention at random.

Then focus on particular poets. Some who are universally recognized as great writers wrote specifically to illuminate the Christian faith. Try the 17th-century poet John Donne (start with the defiant resurrection poem 'Death be not proud'), Gerard Manley Hopkins (a 19th-century Jesuit who composed the ecstatic praise of 'God's Grandeur'), Emily Dickinson (an American poet of the 19th century whose short, simple verses, such as 'The Only News I Know', glimpse heavenly truths), or the recent poet R.S. Thomas (a Welsh clergyman whose fiercely sublime poems, such as 'The Coming', articulate this generation's faith which longs for assurance and wrestles with doubt).

HOW EXTREME?

Here → ① **❷** ③ ④ ⑤ → Heaven

What should I expect?

As you read the shorter pieces, ask yourself why the writer chose poetry, rather than prose, to say this about God. First of all, work out what the words actually mean. Then think about why he or she expressed them in that way. Are there rhymes and rhythms that suggest an orderly creation? Do the sounds of the words soar in a worshipful way, or grind to remind you of humankind's needs? How has the poet used the best words in the best order to give you an inspirational urge to engage with God?

When you progress to reading groups of poems by individual authors, try to work out what their unique style is, and what in God's nature they are inviting us to dwell on. Notice how the content of religious poetry has changed in passing centuries, from the simple certainties of the 16th century ('From this earth, this grave, this dust, My God shall raise me up, I trust', 'The Eve of Execution', Walter Raleigh) to the decline of the sea of faith in the 19th century ('But now I only hear, Its melancholy, long, withdrawing roar', 'Dover Beach', Matthew Arnold).

As you become more at ease with the attention that reading poetry requires, try some of the longer poems, becoming intrigued by the story they tell, being aware of the changing moods they create, and savouring the fact that every word was chosen by the poet in preference to a dozen alternatives. Let the ideas resonate with what you know of the Bible, of worship and of life, and let phrases burrow into your memory to uplift you in subsequent days.

How much?

The Lion Book of Christian Poetry costs £8.99, and *The New Oxford Book of Religious Verse* costs £10.50.

Set aside half an hour on the first occasion, but later be ready to get lost in the poetry as hours go by.

You are most likely to think

These words about God, honoured by passing time, touch my soul because they are richer than anything I could have thought by myself.

You are least likely to think

A poem isn't worth my time,
Unless the lines end with a rhyme,
And nothing useful rhymes with God,
But pod and cod and sod and odd.

Don't!

Don't type 'Christian poetry' into a search engine, because it will generate an avalanche of homespun verse that, although well-meaning, is sentimental and of a poor standard.

Who says?

The transcendent is alive and well in the hands of contemporary poets, despite reports to the contrary, and a dazzling array of poems will appeal in equal measure to religious and literary readers.
David Impastato, poet and anthologist

To help you reflect

The Teacher searched to find just the right words, and what he wrote was upright and true. The words of the wise are like goads, their collected sayings like firmly embedded nails – given by one Shepherd.
Ecclesiastes 12.10, 11

Pleasant words are a honeycomb, sweet to the soul and healing to the bones.
Proverbs 16.24

The date I read religious poetry

Poets that made an impression on me

A line that strikes me as beautiful and true

What I will remember between here and heaven

69 Watch a different kind of movie

HOW? If the films you usually see are in English, choose one that is in a foreign language and has subtitles. If they are usually made in Hollywood, choose one from Iran, Bollywood, France, or one of the other major centres of world cinema – even seeing a British film may stretch your experience. If they are usually in colour, watch a black and white film, or one from the era of silent movies. Or perhaps go to see a film in a genre that is new to you – for example, animation, science fiction or documentary. Then try to put preconceptions out of your mind and surrender to the story.

To find a suitable film, read the reviews in broadsheet newspapers, or a listings magazine such as *Time Out*. Select a film in the knowledge that an expert thinks it has real worth, and watch it asking yourself why he or she saw virtue in it. Alternatively, go to a movie that has been chosen to be shown at a film festival, knowing that a panel has already selected it on its merits.

HOW EXTREME?

Here → ① ❷ ③ ④ ⑤ → Heaven

What should I expect?

Enthusiasts of film, whether or not they are looking at the movies from a Christian perspective, recognize cinemas as secular churches. Diverse people come together and have an experience that fills them with emotion and wonder, and makes them think deeply about the nature of the world they live in – some of the functions of a church service. Unlike churches, cinemas cannot build community, but by bringing people into the same room to have a shared and focused experience, a film can be as powerful spiritually as a service.

The reason for seeing a different kind of movie is that you will watch it with a different set of expectations. You will find yourself thinking about the predicaments of characters, rather than the performances of film stars. If you come out crying, what does the story you have seen tell you about God's activity in the world? If it is a feel-good movie, what does the story you have seen strengthen you to do in order to make the world a place of hope? Instead of the fleeting fun of a typical evening at the cinema, ask yourself how the light that turned into images on the screen can enlighten you.

Don't!

Don't settle for second-best by watching a DVD on television. See the film at its best, on a large screen, in the dark and with no distractions.

£5 to £12, with tickets for special screenings at festivals costing most and afternoon showings at out-of-town cinemas costing least.

 Two to three hours.

How much?

You are most likely to think

Because that film required more concentration than usual, I have had an experience that has more meaning.

You are least likely to think

The popcorn was more nourishing than the film.

To help you reflect

Whatever is true, whatever is noble, whatever is right, whatever is pure, whatever is lovely, whatever is admirable – if anything is excellent or praiseworthy – think about such things.
Philippians 4.8

[God] has made everything beautiful in its time. He has also set eternity in the human heart; yet people cannot fathom what God has done from beginning to end. I know that there is nothing better for people than to be happy and do good while they live. That each of them may eat and drink, and find satisfaction in all their toil – this is the gift of God.
Ecclesiastes 3.11–13

Who says?

Things happen to me in the cinema that should have happened to me in church. It is where I find my sense of what is possible. I want to tell people of faith that they can encounter God everywhere.
Gareth Higgins, film critic

 The date I saw a different kind of film

 Its title

 In what way did it differ from the kinds of entertainment I usually choose?

What I will remember between here and heaven

139

70 Invite your neighbours for a meal

HOW? For some people, inviting those who live on the same street into their homes is so natural that to give instructions for how to do it is insulting. Others struggle even to remember the names of people they see occasionally and wave to in the street. Having become neighbours, the sooner you offer hospitality, the easier it will be to do so. As time goes on, it becomes more difficult to knock on someone's door and invite them for a meal without giving the impression that you have a specific reason for doing so beyond simple neighbourliness. If that is the case, take advantage of an occasion when circumstances bring you into conversation naturally (such as sweeping the communal area of flats, or tidying the garden) to make an invitation.

Select food that allows you to give maximum attention to your guests and minimum attention to preparing the meal. Always choose something that you have cooked before (so that you are not anxious that it might go wrong) and something straightforward (so that your guests will not feel it would be burdensome to invite you back). Ask them in advance whether they have any particular dietary requirements. Do not stretch yourself beyond what you are confident to offer – a good experience of morning coffee and cake is better than an evening meal of three grim courses. Have in mind the first thing you will say to begin conversation, and then relax as you talk.

HOW EXTREME?

Here → ① ❷ ③ ④ ⑤ → Heaven

What should I expect?

Some people know so little about their neighbours that it is possible that Jesus Christ is alive in the house next door, and they are missing the opportunity to befriend him. Offering hospitality brings a new experience of God into your home, and having a meal together allows you to treat a neighbour as if you are serving Jesus – with generosity but without obsequiousness.

Living close to each other inevitably brings difficulties because noise, smells and weather do not respect boundaries. If the most notable conversations you have with neighbours address problems, it puts a great strain on your ability to witness to God's love. However, if there is an easy camaraderie between you, there is a context in which troubles can become opportunities.

Look for what is good and godly in the people. Ask questions that they will take pleasure in answering – about times when they have been happiest, and places they have enjoyed. Listen to everything they say as if it matters a great deal, and remember it. You may be surprised to find that if you make a point of noticing the image of God in other people, they will glimpse the image of God in you without realizing it. You will have taken part in the most effortless and enjoyable evangelism, even though the name of Jesus may never be mentioned.

How much?

Allow £6 per person for a meal that is enjoyable, but not extravagant.

Two hours, plus time spent shopping and preparing food.

You are most likely to think

Somebody extravagantly and uniquely loved by God lives next door to me, and I hadn't realized it until today.

You are least likely to think

I'm moving house.

Don't!

Don't set out with the aim of suggesting that your neighbours come to a church activity. When your friendship has grown to the point at which they invite you to their favourite places, you will be in a comfortable position to invite them to come with you to church.

Who says?

Christians should offer their brethren simple and unpretentious hospitality.
Basil, bishop of Cappadocia (modern Turkey), 330–379

To help you reflect

Share with God's people who are in need. Practise hospitality . . . Rejoice with those who rejoice; mourn with those who mourn. Live in harmony with one another.
Romans 12.13, 15, 16

Keep on loving each other as brothers. Do not forget to entertain strangers, for by so doing some people have entertained angels without knowing it.
Hebrews 13.1, 2

The date I invited my neighbours for a meal

What we ate

What we talked about

What I will remember between here and heaven

71 Change the way you shop

HOW? Altering the way you shop in order to improve the world involves a multitude of small changes. Buying fairly traded food is the simplest start, since most supermarkets stock a reasonable range. Fairly traded clothes, flowers and footballs are harder to find, but progressively more visible. The Fairtrade Foundation publishes a list of stockists on its website (visit www.fairtrade.org.uk, and click 'Suppliers', then 'Retailers' on the left of the page).

Organic food is also increasingly easy to find without changing the location in which you shop. However, there are good reasons to buy more local produce from independent shops, and less food that has been flown wastefully around the world. The decisions are sometimes confusing. Eating a banana from the Caribbean makes a positive contribution to helping poor farmers, but buying foreign strawberries in January involves environmentally destructive freight and it is better to wait until July when local ones are delicious. *The Rough Guide to Ethical Shopping* and the website www.ethicalconsumer.org help you make informed choices (click 'Ten tips' in the second column).

HOW EXTREME?

Here → ① ② ③ ❹ ⑤ → Heaven

What should I expect?

Whenever you get a bargain, someone has subsidized it. Sometimes the shop's marketing strategy has paid for your good fortune, but more often it has passed the expense of your bargain on to a farmer in the developing world who earns about 80p a day and is under pressure to drop his prices. Goods with the Fairtrade logo have been bought from a producer who has been guaranteed a minimum price, and there will also be an extra premium that is invested in the education or health of the community.

It is scandalous that as a result of the way we shop, mothers in the developing world are overcome by poverty and watch their children die of trivial diseases. When you buy fairly traded produce, or organic or local food that has not damaged the environment, you are making a statement that you believe other people's children deserve to thrive as much as your children. It demonstrates, in action rather than mere words, that you believe all people are loved and valued equally by God.

Don't!

Don't worry if you can't do everything at once. If you start with determination you will get an increasing taste for doing what is good until it becomes second nature.

Food that is fairly traded, organic or local costs more. For example, fairly traded coffee costs £2.69 for 227g, instead of £2.49 for coffee that involves farmers suffering. This is not because fairly traded food is unreasonably expensive, but because other food is unreasonably cheap. To keep your expenditure under control, you always have the option of buying less. *The Rough Guide to Ethical Shopping* costs £7.99.

You may have to spend more time shopping, because you will not have the convenience of buying everything at one checkout.

 You are most likely to think

What's that strange, new flavour? Goodness!

 You are least likely to think

I could murder an Indian.

 Who says?

Buy ethical! Buy fair trade! Buy organic! Buy local independent! Buy less! It really annoys me that the only way to get listened to is to spend money, but choosing who gets my money does make an eensy-weensy difference. And some suppliers are worth supporting and fairly traded coffee is actually very nice. That's why I do it. One person can't make a worldwide difference, but the alternative is not doing anything, and that's worse!
Laura Grimoldby, campaigner and commentator

To help you reflect

Hear this, you who trample the needy . . . skimping the measure, boosting the price and cheating with dishonest scales, buying the poor with silver and the needy for a pair of sandals, selling even the sweepings with the wheat. The Lord has sworn . . . 'I will never forget anything they have done.'
Amos 8.4–7

All your ways seem right to you, but the Lord weighs the heart. To do what is right and just is more acceptable to the Lord than sacrifice.
Proverbs 21.2, 3

The date I changed the way I shop

What I have stopped doing, and what I do instead

What I have noticed about the quality

What I will remember between here and heaven

72 Take some exercise

HOW? Start by changing bad habits – use stairs instead of a lift, walk to the corner shop instead of getting in a car, and adjust the television at the set instead of using the remote control. Then consider how you might improve your fitness by taking exercise regularly. The first choice is between taking up a competitive sport (such as joining a football or netball team), or a fitness routine (such as swimming or aerobics).

To find a place where you can play a sport, visit www.sportcom.co.uk, and click on the map of the UK to find where about 50 different sports are played locally by amateurs. To find advice on how to set yourself a fitness programme, visit www.netfit.co.uk, and click on 'gym exercises' and 'workouts'. There you will find 30 different programmes to encourage you to swim, walk, skip, cycle, and so on. You can choose an exercise that suits you, and specialist routines if you are older, pregnant, or want to exercise in your own home.

HOW EXTREME?

Here → ① ② ❸ ④ ⑤ → Heaven

What should I expect?

The writers of the New Testament were concerned for the physical health of young Christians as well as their spirituality. John wrote that he was praying that Gaius would have a body as healthy as his soul. The Christian attitude was that the body was a 'temple' – very different from the prevailing Greek attitude, which was that the body was an evil thing inside which a glorious soul was trapped. So getting fit is a way of honouring the body that God has given you. Exercise is more than just a leisure pursuit; it is a way that God has provided to make you comfortable inside your own skin. Regular exercise means that you will sleep better, feel less stress, and have fewer irritating aches and sniffles. As these things improve, you will find that you enjoy life more, and that is by far the best context in which to love and serve God.

Who says?

Swimming [is] my classroom where God teaches me so much about his ability, and [to have] faith in him. I love the sense of satisfaction that I get when I've done a swimming workout or race, and know that I gave my whole being and heart to God in every moment of the swim. It's the best worship I can offer him.
Penny Heyns, 1996 Olympic breast stroke gold medallist

The cost varies enormously. Walking or running in the neighbourhood costs nothing, although paying £50–£70 for shoes that will give you proper support is a good investment (whereas any old T-shirt and shorts will do). A visit to a public swimming pool costs just over £3 (and is cheaper if you swim regularly). A sports team that plays in a local league might have an annual subscription of about £20, plus a fee of £5 for each match. Prices for an exercise bike range from £150 to £750. Membership of a gym starts at £500 per year, but can soar.

Experts suggest exercising three times per week for at least 20–30 minutes (after 20 minutes your body increases the proportion of energy it takes from your body fat, making you leaner and fitter).

Don't!

Don't take exercise without consulting a doctor if you have any doubts about whether your health is suited to physical activity.

✴ You are most likely to think

I'm not just fitter; I'm happier. That gives me even more reason to praise God.

🌑 You are least likely to think

I'm sure the opposite sex secretly finds a handful of flab attractive.

To help you reflect

Do you not know that your body is a temple of the Holy Spirit, who is in you, whom you have received from God? You are not your own; you were bought at a price. Therefore honour God with your body.
1 Corinthians 6.19, 20

Physical training is of some value, but godliness has value for all things, holding promise for both the present life and the life to come.
1 Timothy 4.8

	The date I started to take exercise seriously

	What activity?

	How I plan to make this a regular event

	What I will remember between here and heaven

73 Observe Ash Wednesday

HOW? Ash Wednesday is the first day of Lent and it is observed 46 days before Easter. Lent has historically been treated as a period in which to examine your life, be aware of behaviour that is leading you away from God's standards, and make changes.

During many Ash Wednesday services, churchgoers have ashes smeared on their foreheads in the shape of a cross. This is a symbol of penitence and awareness of death. It is designed to be on display for the rest of the day, with Christians taking the sign of the cross into the world. The minister uses the words: 'Remember you are dust, and to dust you shall return.' Traditionally the ashes are made by burning palm crosses from the previous year, and mixing them with anointing oil.

Find the date of Ash Wednesday in the 'Holidays by religion' section of www.earthcalendar.net. Contact local churches and find out the time of their Ash Wednesday service. Ask whether the service includes the imposition of ashes, since not all churches follow this ritual.

HOW EXTREME?

Here → ① **❷** ③ ④ ⑤ → Heaven

What should I expect?

Lent is important because only by being aware of the damage of sin and the certainty of death can you fully rejoice on Easter Sunday that sin is forgiven and death overwhelmed by resurrection.

The image of an ashen cross picks up many strands from the Bible. The stories of creation that begin the Bible picture God forming Adam, the prototype human, from dust. The practice of the Jews in the face of calamity or remorse was to wear clothes made from sackcloth (austere and uncomfortable goat's hair) and cover their faces with ash from a dead fire. Ash also alludes to the burning of animals that formed part of the Jewish ritual of seeking God's forgiveness through sacrifice. However, seeing the ash in the form of a cross should remind you, with relief and joy, that because of the death and resurrection of Jesus a sacrifice like that will never be needed again.

Without God, human beings would be nothing more than lifeless dust, and without the cross, humans would anticipate death as nothing more than disintegration. So the solemnity of Ash Wednesday is part of a cycle of sorrow and joy, failure and forgiveness, death and life, that makes up the experience of a believer and is reflected in the calendar of the Christian Church.

If you continue to wear the ashes on your forehead during the day you will almost certainly catch the eye of passers-by who will either be curious, sarcastic, or assume that you are dirty. All those reactions are insignificant in comparison to the response of passers-by to Jesus on his way to the cross, but they may help you recall what forgiveness has cost.

146

How much?

Nothing.

Many churches have services of about 40 minutes in the early morning, but practices vary.

You are most likely to think

Why is everyone looking at me? Oh yes, I remember!

You are least likely to think

Shall I take up smoking for Lent?

Don't!

Don't absent-mindedly wash.

Who says?

We therefore commit this body to the ground; earth to earth, ashes to ashes, dust to dust; in sure and certain hope of the resurrection to eternal life, through our Lord Jesus Christ, who shall change our vile body, that it may be like unto his glorious body.
The Book of Common Prayer: interment prayers from the service for the burial of the dead

To help you reflect

[God said to Adam:] 'By the sweat of your brow you will eat your food until you return to the ground, since from it you were taken; for dust you are and to dust you will return.'
Genesis 3.19

Repent, then, and turn to God, so that your sins may be wiped out [and] that times of refreshing may come from the Lord.
Acts 3.19

The date I observed Ash Wednesday

The church where the ashes were imposed

Reactions to the ash on my forehead during the day

What I will remember between here and heaven

74 Go skinny-dipping

HOW? There are about 50 beaches in the UK where skinny-dipping is encouraged. Descriptions and details of how to reach them can be found by clicking on 'Beaches' at www.british-naturism.org.uk. There are, of course, many circumstances in which it is illegal to be naked in public – usually because the context suggests sexual aggression or is calculated to offend. Because of that, it is impossible for this book to recommend the romance and liberation of swimming nude at midnight in secluded waterfalls and remote lakes with the moon gleaming overhead. Oh well!

Choose a picturesque and isolated location. Make a base with your companions near the water. Gee each other up, count down from ten, rip your clothes off, and sprint into the water. Have plenty of towels and thick clothes available, so that you can get dry and warm quickly when you emerge.

HOW EXTREME?

Here → ① ② ③ ④ ❺ → Heaven

What should I expect?

As you get over the cold and start to enjoy the physical sensation, you will relax more and more about being undressed. The sense of daring that is common immediately before skinny-dipping gives way to a feeling of being embraced, enlivened and at home in your own body (even if it is a body that has more than its share of imperfections).

Most people find skinny-dipping a very pleasant sensation indeed, and it gives them an increased respect for the human body in which God has placed us. Your sense of self-worth will grow as you realize that in the water, without the clothes and accessories that give away everyone's status, you are all equally important and equally humble. This is how God sees you. To have thoughts like these at a moment when the physical sensation is so exhilarating is extremely uplifting. Reflecting on the event later, you may find yourself aware of the great dignity that God conferred on the human body by choosing to inhabit one when he was born as Jesus. That includes every kind of body – male and female, disabled or able-bodied, conventionally good-looking or not.

The freedom of being innocently immersed in God's creation connects you to the first time you were naked in public – when you were born. This can also be invigorating. It is, however, extremely unlikely to be erotic or titillating. Unlike skimpy clothing that is designed to draw attention to a person's sexuality, nudity in this context is more likely to accentuate someone's humanity. So you will become aware of your closeness to a loving God as you realize the goodness of being in his image.

 Nothing.

 On most days in British locations, the temperature is going to mean that this will be a quick dash. Enjoy a longer swim in hotter countries, with all the usual precautions against sunburn.

 Who says?

What spirit is so empty and blind, that it cannot recognize the fact that the foot is more noble than the shoe, and the skin more beautiful than the garment with which it is clothed?
Michelangelo, artist, 1475–1564

 You are most likely to think

Oh b-b-boy, that's cold!

 You are least likely to think

There is something sexual about this.

Don't!

Don't get arrested! And don't decide to do this under the influence of alcohol, which increases the danger at the same time as it decreases the inhibitions.

To help you reflect

The Lord God caused the man to fall into a deep sleep; and while he was sleeping, he took one of the man's ribs and closed up the place with flesh. Then the Lord God made a woman from the rib he had taken out of the man, and he brought her to the man . . . The man and his wife were both naked, and they felt no shame.
Genesis 2.21–25

You created my inmost being;
you knit me together in my mother's womb.
I praise you because I am fearfully and
*   wonderfully made;*
your works are wonderful, I know that full well.
Psalm 139.13–14

The date I went skinny-dipping

Which stretch of water?

Who was there and what made us decide to do it?

What I will remember between here and heaven

149

75 Visit an art gallery

HOW? Visit www.artguide.org and use the search facility of their 'Museums guide' to find an art gallery near you and its opening times. You do not need to book in advance; just turn up. Go slowly, and afterwards sit down in the café to think about what you have seen.

HOW EXTREME?

Here → ① ❷ ③ ④ ⑤ → Heaven

What should I expect?

There is no correct order in which to look at the paintings or sculptures. Drift from room to room, glancing at everything, but stopping and looking closely at works that seem interesting for any reason. In front of these, spend time making sure that you have examined every part of the piece.

Ask yourself: Is it a representation of something, or is it completely abstract? Is it telling a story or evoking a feeling? What can I see that I wouldn't be aware of if this were just a photograph? What is the mood of the piece, and how has the artist used colour, shape and composition to achieve that? Why did the artist choose this medium and this view?

After looking at the picture or sculpture (not before), read the label and find out the title, what it is made of, and when it was created. Sometimes there are also comments about the piece by an art expert. Having read them, look again at the artwork and ask yourself whether they have added to your understanding.

Next, look closely and work out how the artist made the piece. (Where did he use a thick brush and where a small one? How did he or she achieve the details? What tools were used to sculpt or construct?)

Finally, step back again and take in the work as a whole. What is its spiritual mood? Does it give off joy? Anger? Mystery? Pointlessness? Is it a religious piece (either portraying the Christian tradition or giving an insight into an aspect of what it means to be human)? Has it added anything to your inner world? If God had not invented words, might he communicate something through this?

Keep wandering, stopping at some pieces not just to see them, but to look at them. And at the end, reflect on which one you would take away with you if you were offered the choice. Buy a postcard of it in the shop before you go.

Don't!

Don't try to see everything in the gallery or you will get exhausted and stop enjoying it.

How much? The national collections are open to the public free of charge, so you should be able to visit an art gallery without any cost in most of the UK's large cities. Some private galleries and special exhibitions of particular painters have a charge of between £4 and £8.

 If you are visiting for the first time, allow an hour. It will not be enough to see all that is on show, but after that you will start to forget which works you enjoyed.

 Who says?

Art washes the dust of everyday life from your soul.
Pablo Picasso, artist, 1881–1973

 You are most likely to think

There are some thoughts that can't be expressed in a sentence. Maybe God can tell me something through my eyes and feelings that I would never understand through words.

 You are least likely to think

I could have done that. (If you do think it, the fact is that you didn't do it, did you!)

To help you reflect

The Lord has chosen Bezalel son of Uri . . . and he has filled him with the Spirit of God, with skill, ability and knowledge in all kinds of crafts – to make artistic designs for work in gold, silver and bronze, to cut and set stones, to work in wood and to engage in all kinds of artistic craftsmanship.
Exodus 35.30–33

Since the creation of the world God's invisible qualities – his eternal power and divine nature – have been clearly seen, being understood from what has been made.
Romans 1.20

	The date I visited an art gallery

	Where?

	Which works of art made an impact on me?

	What I will remember between here and heaven

76 Fast for a day

HOW? If you have never fasted before, attempt a 24-hour fast from lunch to lunch (missing two meals). During that time eat no food, but drink plenty of water, and perhaps fruit juice. If your family circumstances permit it, pray or read the Bible during meal times. As you notice physical sensations that you are not used to, remind yourself that you are doing this as a sign between you and God that this is a special occasion. Use it to ask him to direct you. Pray, confess or be thankful for something significant. Be aware of the injustice of the world that leaves millions permanently hungry. You will feel best if you end your fast by eating salad, fruit and bread, rather than a heavy meal.

HOW EXTREME?

Here → ① ② ❸ ④ ⑤ → Heaven

What should I expect?

To begin with you will find the physical aspects of what you are doing interesting, but try to monitor your inner attitudes as well, and be aware of what God brings into your mind. Fasting is not magical, and certainly not a way of twisting God's arm. It is, however, a way of prioritizing things that need your attention, knowing that they are already of great concern to God.

You will probably feel hungry at some points. This is not real hunger, however. It is your body responding to the fact that you have conditioned it to expect to receive food at certain points during each day. If you decide not to eat at that point, it is a way of expressing your willingness to let God be in control of your life. Every mundane activity of your normal day is being done with this act of worship going on as its backdrop.

You will find yourself relating the fast to other areas of your life about which you are not content (from irritations on a bus journey to major concerns about relationships). Ask God to help you sort the trivial from the vital, and open yourself to his guidance. You will also be aware of the difference between your desire for food and the very different predicament of those who are hungry because of poverty. This too will make you reconsider your priorities, and may result in decisions that will change you. In all these cases, God will be revealing to you, body and soul, what it means to surrender yourself to him.

How much?

Nothing.

You will neither spend nor save time, but you will be aware in a new way of how the time passes.

Don't!

Don't fast if you are pregnant, diabetic or receiving treatment for a heart condition. If you are in any doubt as to whether this would injure your health, ask your doctor. Don't embarrass friends by turning up to a dinner party and announcing that you won't eat any of the food they have prepared. And don't stuff yourself with food before or after the fast, because that will give unpleasant physical sensations during what should be a very positive experience.

 Who says?

What the eyes are for the outer world, a fast is for the inner world.
Mahatma Gandhi, Indian statesman, 1869–1948

 You are most likely to think

God is my absolute priority at this moment, and the physical feelings inside me keep reminding me that there is a great deal that I need to sort out with him.

 You are least likely to think

The thing the world needs most is more fast food outlets.

To help you reflect

'You eat, but never have enough. You drink, but never have your fill. You put on clothes, but are not warm. You earn wages, only to put them in a purse with holes in it.' This is what the Lord Almighty says: 'Give careful thought to your ways.'
Haggai 1.6, 7

'Everything is permissible for me' – but not everything is beneficial. 'Everything is permissible for me' – but I will not be mastered by anything.
1 Corinthians 6.12

	The date on which I fasted

	What I did with the time when I would usually be eating

	Adjectives that describe my feelings at various stages

	What I will remember between here and heaven

153

77 Send a virtual gift

HOW? When you send a virtual gift to a friend, a charity sends a colourful card to him or her, but uses the majority of the money you have spent to make a substantial improvement to someone's life in one of the world's poorest communities, usually in the developing world. This might be livestock (for instance a beehive), training (such as teaching a specialist to clear landmines), or health care (a mosquito net that prevents malaria).

Catalogues, such as Present Aid (from PO Box 100, London, SE1 7RT), appear as Christmas approaches and suggest gifts at a range of prices. The card, which shows a picture of the kind of gift you have chosen and explains where it will be sent, can be sent directly to the recipient, or to you, so that you can give it in person. At the website, www.presentaid.org, it is also possible to create a list of virtual presents you would like to receive to mark a special occasion. You can then encourage friends to choose from the list instead of giving you a more conventional gift. Send a Cow has a similar scheme (www.sendacow.org.uk). At www.giveit.co.uk it is possible to set up an alternative Christmas or wedding list, benefiting a wide selection of charities working with poor or vulnerable people in the UK and the developing world.

HOW EXTREME?

Here → **①** ② ③ ④ ⑤ → Heaven

What should I expect?

An operation to restore the sight of a blind person in India costs about the same as giving someone a pair of designer pants. Almost anyone can appreciate which of those has a more lasting value. The joy of a virtual gift is that it shows someone you love that you thought specifically of them, and imaginatively matched them up with an appropriate present. They feel appreciated, you know that you haven't been trapped into wasting money by the commercialism of Christmas, and someone in the developing world will have their life transformed.

Sending a virtual gift is one of the few ways of giving to charity that guarantees cheerfulness, and because the Bible tells us that God loves a cheerful giver, we know that even he shares in the rejoicing. Giving generously to needy people reflects the actions of Jesus, who gave himself to be born in great humility instead of in a palace.

How much?

Gifts that benefit charities range from £7 (a stethoscope to be used in Cambodia) to £790 (concrete to build a well in Mali). The most popular gift from Present Aid is a can of worms (for composting on farms in the poorest parts of Bolivia, costing £15). A consistently popular one from the Alternative Christmas List is a goat (providing an African family with milk, manure and kids to sell, costing £27).

About 20 minutes to browse, choose and pay. A card to send to the recipient arrives three days later.

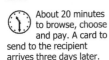 **Who says?**

You can give without loving, but you cannot love without giving.
Amy Carmichael, missionary to Asia, 1867–1951

 You are most likely to think

These are the most worthwhile presents I have ever purchased.

You are least likely to think

Should I have given them socks instead?

Don't!

Don't give a virtual present to someone who might mistakenly interpret your great concern for the world's poorest people as a sign that you don't care for them sufficiently to buy a more usual gift.

To help you reflect

Each of you should give what you have decided in your heart to give, not reluctantly or under compulsion, for God loves a cheerful giver. And God is able to make all grace abound to you, so that in all things at all times, having all that you need, you will abound in every good work. As it is written: 'They have scattered abroad their gifts to the poor; their righteousness endures for ever.'
2 Corinthians 9.7–9

One gives freely, yet gains even more; another withholds unduly, but comes to poverty. A generous person will prosper; the one who refreshes others will be refreshed.
Proverbs 11.24, 25

The date I sent a virtual gift

What and to whom?

In which country will people benefit from what I have done?

What I will remember between here and heaven

78 Run a marathon

HOW? A good list of marathons and half-marathons in the UK can be found at www.weightlossresources.co.uk. Click on 'Exercise', then 'Fun runs', and follow the links to the website of one that interests you. The most popular have a ballot for entry (unless you have proven experience); others are open to all. Read the registration instructions carefully, since all are different. The websites give suggested programmes of training, but it is up to you to find the discipline to keep to an arduous schedule over several months. They also explain ways of using the run to generate money for charity.

Most races require you to register in person the day before, where you collect a race number, a kit bag, and a computerized chip to attach to your shoe, which will record your precise time. At the finish, expect a medal, a T-shirt, a massage and a feeling of exhilaration!

HOW EXTREME?

Here → ① ② ③ ④ ❺ → Heaven

What should I expect?

One of the reasons that marathons are popular is that, although they are extremely daunting, they are not impossible. Ordinary people, if they are single-minded, can achieve something extraordinary. The training (a combination of short jogs, increasingly long runs, and rest) is extremely good for your body. The race, while gruelling for your body, is extremely good for your sense of worth. No one will take the achievement from you. And using the race to raise money for charity ensures that your pride in the success is shared generously. In perseverance, joy and pain, it is a model for the whole of a worthwhile Christian life.

How much?

Entry for the Edinburgh marathon (after a ballot) costs £39. The Cardiff marathon (guaranteed entry) costs £26. Charities have places reserved for runners who are able to commit themselves to raising a minimum amount. Typically registration costs £50, and the charity sets a sum between £500 and £2,000 as the target. You must also have shoes suitable for running on roads, costing at least £50–£70.

Organizers suggest training programmes, usually for the 12 weeks before the marathon. They begin with a 30-minute run and then increase, alternating training days and rest days. During the race, most inexperienced runners would regard a time of under 4 hours as a triumph, and under 5 hours as respectable. The world record is 2 hours 4 minutes 55 seconds for men and 2 hours 15 minutes 25 seconds for women.

Don't!

Don't set off so fast that you have to give up (either the training or the event). Like life itself, finishing matters.

You are most likely to think

Having achieved something extremely difficult with God's help, I can look at other difficult things in my life in a more positive way.

You are least likely to think

I think I'll do that again tomorrow.

Who says?

Training for and running the marathon is like having a chance to survey the course of your Christian life – the decision to begin, the challenge to stick with the programme, the victories, the set-backs, the desire to quit conflicting with the desire to endure and reach the ultimate goal. It teaches you that nothing is really achieved without effort. A marathon is completed one step at a time.
James Smith, participant in the Cincinnati 'Flying Pig' marathon

To help you reflect

Do you not know that in a race all the runners run, but only one gets the prize? Run in such a way as to get the prize. Everyone who competes in the games goes into strict training. They do it to get a crown that will not last; but we do it to get a crown that will last for ever.
1 Corinthians 9.24–25

Let us throw off everything that hinders and the sin that so easily entangles, and let us run with perseverance the race marked out for us. Let us fix our eyes on Jesus, the author and perfecter of our faith, who for the joy set before him endured the cross, scorning its shame, and sat down at the right hand of the throne of God.
Hebrews 12.1, 2

The date I ran a marathon

In which city?

My finishing time

What I will remember between here and heaven

157

79 Investigate a saint

HOW? Access a biographical dictionary of saints (hagiography). Examples are published by Oxford University Press and Penguin Books. *Saints on Earth* (Church House Publishing) is a substantial book and CD designed for people who intend to use the information in the context of worship. There is a smaller online dictionary at www.justus.anglican.org (click the 'bio postings' link) that begins with Onesimus (who lived in Colossae soon after the life of Jesus) and ends with Janani Luwum (who died in Uganda in 1977).

Choose to investigate a saint whose name you have heard of – perhaps because his image appears on a stained glass window, a local church is dedicated to her, or because you share a name or a date of birth. Then let your curiosity lead you from saint to saint, and use the internet to research further.

HOW EXTREME?

Here → **❶** ② ③ ④ ⑤ → Heaven

What should I expect?

In the Bible, the word saint is used simply to mean a faithful Christian. The word means 'holy', and can apply to believers who are living or dead. However, the common use of the word is to describe someone from the past whose life was righteous and inspirational. In some traditions there is a process involving research and prayer over many years by which particular people come to be recognized officially as saints (canonization).

Saints are examples to the Christian community of how we should all behave. Their stories are passed on over the years (sometimes retold with such relish that the actual truth of their lives is less interesting than the embellishments) so that future generations will be encouraged and have their faith in God made strong.

Read the story of saints' lives fully aware that the legend may have outgrown the truth, but attempting to understand what virtue there was in the men, women or children that inspired people to want to honour them by preserving the story. What was it about their faith in Jesus Christ that allowed them to achieve more than seems possible to most Christians? What would that kind of devotion look like in a Christian who is alive in this generation? What would you be doing now if you had that kind of character? What's stopping you?

A paperback *Dictionary of Saints* (either Oxford or Penguin) costs £8.99. The price of *Saints on Earth* is £20. The online resources are free.

Begin by allowing 30 minutes, but be prepared for hours to go by if you are intrigued.

You are most likely to think

This was an ordinary Christian person who did ordinary Christian things, but he or she did them very much better than others, and with selfless motives.

You are least likely to think

I'll be on that list one day.

Who says?

Saints are people who make it easier for others to believe in God.
Nathan Söderblom, Archbishop of Uppsala, 1866–1931

Don't!

Don't be anxious about traditions that involve praying to saints. The Holy Spirit's work is to take our prayers to God, made flawless. So all kinds of prayer, no matter how imperfectly we utter them, are received graciously by God. The inspiration you get from the life of a saint may help you pray, so make the most of that, but it cannot make a prayer better or worse. God's response will be perfect, and nothing about your prayer can make him more perfect than perfect!

To help you reflect

Remember your leaders, who spoke the word of God to you. Consider the outcome of their way of life and imitate their faith.
Hebrews 13.7

Some faced jeers and flogging, while still others were chained and put in prison . . . destitute, persecuted and mistreated – the world was not worthy of them. They wandered in deserts and mountains, and in caves and holes in the ground. These were all commended for their faith, yet none of them received what had been promised. God had planned something better for us so that only together with us would they be made perfect.
Hebrews 11.36–40

	The date I investigated the life of a saint

	The name of the saint

	The most interesting thing about his or her life

	What I will remember between here and heaven

80 Run a children's group

HOW? Approach the minister of a church at which you worship and discuss the best place for you to use your skills. Suggest that it might be in a children's group, but be open to the possibility that he or she may have a different suggestion. Visit groups to observe, and consider whether your temperament is more suited to older or younger children. Meanwhile, approach the Criminal Records Bureau to apply for a disclosure (a document that everyone working near children should have to ensure that no one who has hurt a child in the past is exposed to the opportunity again – details at www.disclosure.gov.uk).

When you find a group that you feel you will enjoy, talk to its leader about the possibility of becoming involved. Begin with a small task (such as serving refreshments or chatting with children about what they are doing) and, week by week, increase your involvement by helping children with craft, explaining how to play a game, or reading a Bible story.

Alternatively, volunteer in a secular group and use the same skills to serve children beyond the reach of the church in a godly way.

HOW EXTREME?

Here → ① ② ③ ④ ❺ → Heaven

What should I expect?

Some people begin to help with the expectation that they will tell children about Jesus, but discover that they learn more than they teach. Children hide less than adults. When they are bored, they display it openly. Their questions require straightforward answers. When they are listened to and cared for, they respond with generous love.

Expect to laugh, to be exhausted, to be frustrated when certain children are unco-operative, and to feel young again. Be aware that children shape their view of God by watching you – not only when you are talking about the Christian faith, but also when you are refereeing a game. So treat the group as an opportunity for leaders and children to learn together as they discover and follow Jesus, not as a time to persuade children to respond in a formulaic way.

 Who says?

Let our children partake of the training that is in Christ. Let them learn how humility avails with God, what [his] pure love can do, how the fear of God is good and great and saves those who live therein.
Clement, bishop of Rome, about 35–100

How much?

Any church that takes children seriously will fully cover the cost of running groups for them, so there should be no expense. And any church that doesn't take the needs of children seriously is in its final years.

More than you think! If a children's group runs for an hour, anticipate two to three hours of preparation, pastoral care and prayer.

Don't!

Don't be irregular in attendance, because you need to build up friendships through which children can experience the love of God.

You are most likely to think

I thought that children were important because they are tomorrow's church, but now I realize that they are actually today's church.

You are least likely to think

Running a children's group is so much easier than running an adults' group.

To help you reflect

People were bringing little children to Jesus to have him touch them, but the disciples rebuked them. When Jesus saw this, he was indignant. He said to them, 'Let the little children come to me, and do not hinder them, for the kingdom of God belongs to such as these. I tell you the truth, anyone who will not receive the kingdom of God like a little child will never enter it.' And he took the children in his arms, put his hands on them and blessed them.
Mark 10.13–16

[The Lord] commanded our forefathers to teach
*   their children,*
so the next generation would know them,
even the children yet to be born,
and they in turn would tell their children.
Then they would put their trust in God
and would not forget his deeds but would keep his
*   commands.*
Psalm 78.5–7

The date I helped run a children's group for the first time

The name of the group

What activities took place?

What I will remember between here and heaven

81 Pray in an airport

HOW? All the large airports in the UK, and some smaller ones, have a chapel. Often the room is a space for prayer shared by several faiths. The pattern across the world varies (widespread in the USA, but rare in Australia). Even in places where there is no chapel, airports tend to have a chaplain. A substantial list of opening hours and telephone numbers is maintained at www.misas.org/paises/aeropuertos.html.

Airport chapels tend to be plain, comfortable and sensitively lit. Most are open and untended from morning to evening, and have a notice giving the times of occasional services and details of how to contact the chaplain. They can be used for personal prayer, but chaplains will pray with groups before they travel together or with individuals. In many airports, Christian staff meet for prayer and fellowship. On the rare occasions when airports become gathering places following an accident, chaplains are key to the pastoral care.

HOW EXTREME?

Here → ① ❷ ③ ④ ⑤ → Heaven

What should I expect?

Airport terminals are large and disorienting places. They have the features of shopping centres, with attention-grabbing displays. Airport chapels are designed to contrast completely. They are uncluttered, relaxing and have a human scale. They are kept simple so that everyone can share them. Most do not have religious symbols in recognition that airports are gathering points for people of all the world's religions. It is acceptable for Christians to bring their own symbols with them.

Moving from the commotion of a terminal into the quiet of a chapel unveils an airport's best-kept secret. Before travelling at great speed, slow down to a point at which you are very still. In this place through which people of every nationality pass, take the opportunity to think about what it means to be in the care of the God who is creator of the heavens as well as the earth, and of every religion of humankind as well as the Christians. If you are nervous of flying, use the tranquillity to commit the journey to God, knowing that he will accompany you through the turbulence in as real a way as he is with you in the calm.

How much?

 Nothing.

You have time for a few seconds of peace if you are waiting for a domestic flight; on a long-haul flight with a substantial check-in time you could attend a service of ten to 20 minutes.

Don't!

Don't underestimate how long it will take to reach your plane.

Who says?

My parish is the largest in the world – 61 million people visited it in the past twelve months. Conversely, attendances at services must be among the lowest – eight on Easter Sunday. There is a chapel and a multifaith prayer room – light, comfortable and plain . . . My job is to knock on doors and talk to strangers. I see myself as the last outpost of unashamed Anglican ministry . . . For passengers frightened to fly, refugees, those meeting and greeting, stressed-out staff from the police, airlines and hotels, I keep the faith flying.
David Smith, former chaplain to Heathrow Airport

You are most likely to think

In this bustling place I have momentarily slowed down to a pace at which I can meet God, and now I am conscious that his blessing will be with me above the clouds.

You are least likely to think

What they most need here is another outlet for cheap booze and fags.

To help you reflect

Where can I go from your Spirit?
Where can I flee from your presence?
If I go up to the heavens, you are there;
if I make my bed in the depths, you are there.
If I rise on the wings of the dawn,
if I settle on the far side of the sea,
even there your hand will guide me,
your right hand will hold me fast.
Psalm 139.7–10

Great is your love, higher than the heavens;
your faithfulness reaches to the skies.
Be exalted, O God, above the heavens,
and let your glory be over all the earth.
Psalm 108.4, 5

The date I prayed in an airport

The name of the airport and my destination

What I prayed about

What I will remember between here and heaven

82 Read the Bible from cover to cover

HOW? The most straightforward way to read the Bible is to start at the first book, Genesis, and read a chapter every day. There are, however, disadvantages to reading the Bible in this way. The later books speak to the spirit of a Christian in a much more vital way than those at the start, but it will take two and a half years to reach the part about the life of Jesus! And the Bible books are ordered in a way that keeps the various genres (prophecy, letters, laws, and so on) together, which does not lend itself to variety if you are reading from beginning to end.

There are several alternative ways of reading the whole Bible, most of which involve reading about three chapters daily. It is possible to follow a scheme that allows you to read the Bible in chronological order, so that the unfolding story of God's dealings with humankind becomes clear. Or you can read it in the order in which the books may have been written. Other schemes allow you to read part of the Old Testament and part of the New Testament every day, sometimes yielding unexpected insights and comparisons. You can find published schemes in a Christian bookshop or by clicking on 'Bible reading plans' at www.backtothebible.org/devotions.

HOW EXTREME?

Here → ① ② ❸ ④ ⑤ → Heaven

What should I expect?

Reading the Bible has a slow, cumulative effect. Its value doesn't enter the bloodstream quickly and headily like alcohol. Instead it slowly seeps into your life like vitamins. When you read the entire Bible, it becomes less likely that a single sentence or issue from it will dominate the way you view your faith, and more likely that you will become engrossed by the vast scale of the project on which God is working.

With each chapter, ask yourself what kind of literature you are reading. Is it someone's life story? (If so, should you be following their good example or treating their failure as a warning?) Is it advice given to an ancient people about how to be godly? (If so, what would be the equivalent advice to those in our very different generation who want to be equally godly?) Is it poetic language? (If so, can God touch you through it in a way that a newspaper cannot?)

Some things you will find shocking. Let them anger you! Some things you will find inspiring. Enjoy the exhilaration! Do not be dispirited by things you cannot understand, but keep reading so that the overall themes of the Bible – love, justice, faith – are the ones that leave their mark on you. (However, if you are so baffled that you find it disturbing, refer to a commentary – a volume that explains the significance of a Bible book verse by verse.)

How much?

A basic edition of the Bible costs between £7 and £15. Alternatively, read it free online at www.biblegateway.com.

Between them the books of the Bible contain 1,189 chapters, so reading three chapters per day (15 minutes) and occasionally four will mean that you have read the entire Bible in a year.

Who says?

Most people are bothered by those passages of Scripture they do not understand. But the parts that bother me are the ones I do understand.
Mark Twain, writer, 1835–1910

You are most likely to think

The words are ancient, but some of them take on startling new significance in the light of events in the 21st century.

You are least likely to think

The sequel is not as good as the first one.

Don't!

Don't give up in the middle of Numbers.

To help you reflect

All Scripture is God-breathed and is useful for teaching, rebuking, correcting and training in righteousness, so that God's servant may be thoroughly equipped for every good work.
2 Timothy 3.16, 17

Everything that was written in the past was written to teach us, so that through endurance and the encouragement of the Scriptures we might have hope.
Romans 15.4

The dates when I began and ended my reading of the Bible

The parts I enjoyed most and least

My feelings at having completed it

What I will remember between here and heaven

83 Make a sharing arrangement

HOW? Begin by identifying things that you need to use only occasionally – say every six months. Among these might be a power drill, a vacuum for Autumn leaves, or a kitchen implement that does a very specific job. Put a message in your local church newsletter or magazine explaining that you own these items and are investigating whether anyone would like to share them, or that you intend to buy something and wonder whether one or two people would like to share the ownership and the cost. If people respond, meet with them and discuss where the objects will be located, and how you can be sure you can all have access to them when they are needed. Record on a piece of paper what it is you are sharing, and the address and phone numbers of all the people involved. Although it is not necessary to sign this as a formal agreement (unless, of course, it is something of great value), discuss what will happen when someone moves house or no longer wants to be part of the agreement, and make a note of it. And then (the most enjoyable part) decide together what to do with the money you have saved. Set it free to be used to do good.

If this proves a success, consider making a similar arrangement for things you use more frequently, bearing in mind that you need to live closer to someone with whom you are sharing tools, a lawn mower, or items that you would use on holiday or when guests come to stay. And if you really get enthusiastic, work on the possibility of making a genuine impact for environmental good by sharing a car, a washing machine, or something else in daily use.

HOW EXTREME?

Here → ① ② ❸ ④ ⑤ → Heaven

What should I expect?

The object of making a sharing agreement is that the good you achieve together substantially outweighs the inconvenience of not having something in your possession every moment of every day. The good includes money released for good causes, and the benefit to the environment of less waste, but also the trust and co-operation that builds friendships.

In the church in Jerusalem during the years after Jesus' resurrection, the way Christians shared their property and lives was so marked that need came to an end in the community. It made such an impression on those who watched it happening that it drew them to faith. Making a sharing arrangement goes so completely against today's culture that it will make a deep impression on people now as then, so make sure that what you are doing is noticed by as many people as possible.

How much?

Nothing, and this may release money to be used for a generous purpose.

Depending on what you share and with whom, you should be prepared for activities to take longer than usual.

You are most likely to think

Sharing has given me deeper friendships as well as saving me money.

You are least likely to think

But I can't possibly manage without a wallpaper stripper of my own.

Don't!

Don't lose track of the agreement you have made, so that you make sure there can never be bad feeling because one of you forgets what you arranged.

Who says?

We are not cisterns made for hoarding; we are channels made for sharing.
Billy Graham, North American evangelist

To help you reflect

Command [those who are well off] to do good, to be rich in good deeds, and to be generous and willing to share. In this way they will lay up treasure for themselves as a firm foundation for the coming age, so that they may take hold of the life that is truly life.
1 Timothy 1.18, 19

All the believers were one in heart and mind. No one claimed that any of their possessions was their own, but they shared everything they had. With great power the apostles continued to testify to the resurrection of the Lord Jesus, and much grace was upon them all. There were no needy persons among them.
Acts 4.32–34

	The date I set up a sharing arrangement
	What and with whom?
	The advantages and disadvantages so far
	What I will remember between here and heaven

84 Visit a nursing home

HOW? Because elderly and sick people are vulnerable, there are safeguards to ensure that visiting a nursing home is a positive experience for everyone concerned. It is not possible to knock unannounced on the front door and ask for immediate access to visit strangers. In the first instance, ask the leaders of your local church whether they have a relationship with residences in the area to which you could contribute.

If the church does not have a pastoral scheme of this kind, make contact with a nursing home and ask whether they would welcome a regular visitor to talk with the residents. If you have special skills, such as hand massage, beauty treatment, music, or leading exercise or worship, explain what you could offer. But initially these are less significant than a willingness to sit and chat. Be ready to make an appointment to speak to the manager and prove your identity. Explain how much time you could offer, and be prepared to fit in with what is needed, rather than imposing your own ideas in an insensitive way.

HOW EXTREME?

Here → ① ② ❸ ④ ⑤ → Heaven

What should I expect?

Most nursing homes warmly welcome regular visitors, because their staff are overstretched by attending to the physical needs of their clients and so people who are able to spend time offering company and friendship improve the lives of guests and workers alike. Some residents have no visitors at all, and a new friendship gives them emotional support, a rhythm to their week, and a sense of dignity. Of course, it may be that there is a reason why they do not have visitors, and the friendship you form can involve spending time melting years of becoming embittered before a person's true personality begins to emerge. However, nearly everyone becomes a better person when they are offered affection, and you should expect to enjoy visiting increasingly as time goes by.

It may be that playing board games or sharing craft (chess or knitting, perhaps) gives a starting point, but also begin conversations about memories and experiences. And if the person has a disability that makes talking difficult, being present in silence is valuable of itself. Remember continuously that the image of God is present in each person and seek it out. What do wrinkles tell you about God's nature? Or deafness? Or gentleness? Or loneliness? In Psalm 71, an ageing man writes, 'Even though I am old and grey, do not forsake me, O God, till I declare your power to the next generation.' You are that next generation! Expect to learn the power of God through your visits.

How much?

 Nothing.

 Spending a little over an hour every week visiting the same home will allow relationships to build, both with staff and residents.

Don't!

Don't begin a friendship with someone and then stop visiting unexpectedly or on whim. Only make commitments that you know you can fulfil.

You are most likely to think

There is a deep wealth of experience and wisdom within the walls of nursing homes, and it is foolishness to waste it.

You are least likely to think

Poor old soul!

To help you reflect

[In a parable, Jesus said:] 'I was hungry and you gave me something to eat, I was thirsty and you gave me something to drink, I was a stranger and you invited me in, I needed clothes and you clothed me, I was sick and you looked after me, I was in prison and you came to visit me . . . I tell you the truth, whatever you did for one of the least of these brothers and sisters of mine, you did for me.'
Matthew 25.35, 36, 40

Religion that God our Father accepts as pure and faultless is this: to look after orphans and widows in their distress and to keep oneself from being polluted by the world.
James 1.27

Who says?

A society which treasures the elderly and disabled, and looks after them, is a generous society. Once this stops, life becomes cheap.
Basil Hume, Roman Catholic archbishop, 1923–1999

	The date I began to visit a nursing home

	The names of the people I talked to

	Something interesting from one of my conversations

What I will remember between here and heaven

85 Collect for a charity

HOW? By far the largest house-to-house collection in Britain and Ireland is for Christian Aid, working in the interests of the world's poorest communities. Smaller collections include the Children's Society (helping children who face harsh challenges) and the British Heart Foundation (combating heart disease). Contact their headquarters to be a volunteer (www.christianaid.org.uk or 020 7523 2270; www.the-childrens-society.org.uk or 0845 300 1128; www.bhf.org.uk or 0800 019 2123). They will put you in touch with local representatives who can explain how the collection works in your area. This local contact is vital, because protecting the collection from fraud relies on money being passed from one trustworthy person to another, each of them knowing the other personally.

A collection usually involves pushing envelopes provided by the charity through 50 to 100 doors at the start of a particular week. Later you return, knock on the door, and ask whether the householder would like to contribute. If they hand you an envelope with money in, ask them to write their name and address in the designated space, which (if they are taxpayers) will mean that the government increases their gift by just under a third. Follow the charity's instructions about what to do in order to get the money to their headquarters.

HOW EXTREME?

Here → ① ② ❸ ④ ⑤ → Heaven

What should I expect?

Collecting for a charity is humbling. Our experience of someone asking us for money is usually limited to a destitute person begging, so when you collect for a charity you show yourself willing to identify with that helplessness. You risk rejection and insult – it is not a pleasant thing to do. It would be easier simply to write a cheque.

However, knocking on doors and making people aware of a pressing need is an act of witness. Its impact goes far beyond the usefulness of the money that is collected, because it announces the values of the Kingdom of God to the neighbourhood. It reminds them that poor people need good news, suffering people need rescue, and unhappy people need peace. This was the work of Jesus, who was humbled to the point of wretchedness, and this is a way of coming alongside him in sacrificial service.

How much?

 Nothing.

For 50 envelopes, allow an hour to distribute them, three hours to collect them with money in, and a further hour to return to homes where there was no reply.

Don't!

Don't let a shower of rain daunt you – people are more generous to a collector who perseveres in adverse conditions.

You are most likely to think

That was tough, but not nearly as tough as the circumstances suffered by the people on whose behalf I was collecting.

You are least likely to think

I have collected sufficient.

Who says?

Christ has no body now on earth but yours, no hands but yours, no feet but yours. Yours are the eyes through which Christ's compassion for the world is to look out; yours are the feet with which he is to go about doing good; yours are the hands with which he is to bless.
Teresa of Avila, abbess and mystic, 1515–1582

To help you reflect

We want you to know about the grace that God has given the Macedonian churches. Out of the most severe trial, their overflowing joy and their extreme poverty welled up in rich generosity. For I testify that they gave as much as they were able, and even beyond their ability. Entirely on their own, they urgently pleaded with us for the privilege of sharing in this service to the saints.
2 Corinthians 8.1–4

[Jesus said,] 'Be careful not to do your "acts of righteousness" before others, to be seen by them . . . When you give to the needy, do not announce it with trumpets, as the hypocrites do in the synagogues and on the streets, to be honoured by others . . . Do not let your left hand know what your right hand is doing, so that your giving may be in secret.'
Matthew 6.1–4

	The date I collected money for charity

	Where?

	How much did you collect and for which charity?

	What I will remember between here and heaven

86 Pray in a cathedral

HOW? Links to the websites of most (but not all) cathedrals in the UK can be found at www.cathedralsplus.org.uk. From them you can find the opening times, which are typically from early morning (a 7.30 service is not unusual) to late afternoon (sometimes closing with a service at 5.30) on both weekdays and Sundays. There are, however, many variations.

There are three ways of praying in a cathedral. Attend a service led by the resident choir, or a shorter spoken service, or use the cathedral at any time for personal prayer. A choral service feels in some ways like an exceptional performance, with the congregation encouraged to join in a few items. A spoken service has a smaller scale, with a greater emphasis on praying for the world. Personal prayer allows you to meet God in a place where many have prayed before you, and the lofty setting gives this a unique feel.

HOW EXTREME?

Here → ① **❷** ③ ④ ⑤ → Heaven

What should I expect?

The scale of the building makes praying in a cathedral unique and, no matter what kind of prayer you engage in, the space has an impact. At a choral service, the magnificent acoustics give the sound of the choir an ethereal quality that will lead you to reflect on the grandeur and holiness of God. The formality of the occasion reflects a desire that everything offered to God in worship over the centuries (the building itself and everything that takes place within) should have an enduring excellence, because that is what he deserves.

As you take part in spoken or silent prayer, the space around you will take on a sense of enveloping godliness, and the echoes will intensify your awareness of the God who listens attentively. Be conscious of the thousands who have prayed in this place before you and (if it is a historic building) the sense of awe and delight that Christians of previous centuries, unused to tall buildings, had as they walked the same paving slabs.

 Who says?

Questions of [human status] recede, for the sheer scale of the building has the power to make anyone feel as insignificant as an ant. This is a place that was designed to change perspective – to make people breathe differently, think differently and act differently just by walking inside.
Rachel Halliburton, writing about St Paul's Cathedral in Time Out

Don't!

Don't run out of patience with tourists who come and go as you pray. They too have been drawn to the cathedral by wanting to experience something out-of-the-ordinary, and that is a response to their spirituality, even if they do not recognize it. If they distract you, pray for them.

How much?

In response to the great expense of keeping cathedrals open, some make a charge for admission to tourists (ranging from £4.80 at Ely to £8 at St Paul's, London). Most are still free, but it would be irresponsible to leave without making a donation. There is no fee for admission to worship, and even those that charge have chapels freely available for personal prayer.

Allow an hour, giving you time to appreciate the scale and beauty before you turn to prayer. The length of cathedral services varies greatly from 20 minutes for a spoken service to 60 minutes for choral evensong (longer at special festivals or if there is a sermon).

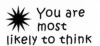 **You are most likely to think**

The Christian faith has a past, a present and a future in this land.

 You are least likely to think

I can't wait to get back out into the traffic.

To help you reflect

How lovely is your dwelling place, O Lord Almighty!
My soul yearns, even faints, for the courts of the Lord;
my heart and my flesh cry out for the living God . . .
Blessed are those who dwell in your house;
they are ever praising you.
Psalm 84.1, 2, 4

Praise the Lord, all you servants of the Lord
who minister by night in the house of the Lord.
Lift up your hands in the sanctuary and praise the Lord.
May the Lord, the Maker of heaven and earth,
bless you from Zion.
Psalm 134.1–3

The date I prayed in a cathedral

Which one?

What I prayed about

What I will remember between here and heaven

173

87 Make a confession

HOW? In the Roman Catholic tradition, priests make themselves available during the hour before Mass to hear people confess what they have done wrong. A structure like a large cupboard with two doors allows you to talk to a priest confidentially through a grille. You will be aware of his presence, but not threatened by it. He will ask what you want to confess (there is a traditional form of words, but a sensitive priest will help you if you do not know how to express yourself). He will suggest what you might do to repair the damage you have done to another person, and what prayers you might say to restore your relationship with God. He will then assure you of God's forgiveness with a sentence of which the crucial words are, 'I absolve you.'

In Protestant traditions, a church leader will listen to you confess sins whose shame you want to be rid of. Some Anglican churches do this in a formal way. In other churches there will be more informality, but all will end with an assurance that you are forgiven, and pastoral advice.

There are circumstances in which confessing to a trusted Christian friend, who understands your circumstances, is more directly helpful. There are also internet sites such as www.dailyconfession.com, on which it is possible to write anonymously (although they tend to attract more confessions of a sexual nature than any other kind).

HOW EXTREME?

Here → ① ② ❸ ④ ⑤ → Heaven

What should I expect?

Doing wrong impedes your ability to live your life to the full, with joyful and peaceful relationships. But God is able to forgive sins so completely that they lose their power to spoil relationships. Forgiveness requires an acknowledgement of the damage you have done, a genuine regret, and a sincere intention not to offend again.

All Christian traditions recognize that only God can forgive sins, so it is to God that you make your confession. However, it is difficult to express your thoughts honestly to God, and revealing the truth to another person, and hearing them say, 'God forgives,' is extremely liberating. Depending on how heavily the burden of having done wrong weighs on you, you may feel relief instantly. But equally you may feel few emotions, and only discover as days go by that you are able to view people you have wronged in a different way.

Nothing.

How much?

Forgiveness is instant. At a Catholic church, the priest will expect to spend 5–10 minutes with you in the confessional, with more time before and after spent in self-examination and prayer. Any church leader will welcome your making an appointment should longer be required.

Who says?

Since the communion of last Easter I have led a life so dissipated and useless, and my terrors and perplexities have so much increased, that I am under great depression and discouragement. Yet I purpose to present myself before God tomorrow, with humble hope that he will not break the bruised reed.
Samuel Johnson, writer, 1709–1784

You are most likely to think

I have taken responsibility for my own actions, and glimpsed myself as God sees me. There is now nothing to stop me putting the past behind me and becoming the person I want to be.

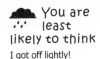

You are least likely to think

I got off lightly!

Don't!

Don't allow confession to grow so routine that the experience becomes trite. It is too important.

To help you reflect

If we claim to be without sin, we deceive ourselves and the truth is not in us. If we confess our sins, he is faithful and just, and will forgive us our sins and purify us from all unrighteousness.
1 John 1.8–10

Day and night your hand was heavy upon me;
my strength was sapped as in the heat of summer.
Then I acknowledged my sin to you
and did not cover up my iniquity.
I said, 'I will confess my transgressions to the Lord,'
and you forgave the guilt of my sin.
Therefore let everyone who is godly
pray to you while you may be found.
Psalm 32.4–6

The date I confessed a sin that had previously been a secret

To whom?

How I felt before and after

What I will remember between here and heaven

88 Dress a well

HOW? The custom of well dressing takes place mainly in Derbyshire. Villages decorate their wells with large, upright floral designs. Although it has its roots in pre-Christian history, it is now used as a Christian act of thanksgiving to God for the water on which we depend.

A wooden tray of several square metres is soaked in a local stream, then packed with clay and salt. A blueprint is created on paper, combining biblical images and words with local references, and the outlines are traced on to the clay with pinpricks. 'Petallers' then fill the design with flowers, mosses, berries and seeds of various colours.

The season lasts from May to September. Each community has its spectacular display in position for about a week, which begins with an act of worship – usually a procession followed by a blessing of the water in the well. The dates are listed at www.welldressing.com.

HOW EXTREME?

Here → ① **❷** ③ ④ ⑤ → Heaven

What should I expect?

The custom was revived and given a Christian context in 1348 in the village of Tissington. It was offered as a thanksgiving to God that the village survived the Black Death, which they attributed to the purity of the water in their wells.

Drinking water is a gift of God that we take for granted. In many countries, collecting the water that is necessary for survival requires a journey of several miles. It is usually the work of girls who, because they have to walk for many hours, are not able to go to school, trapping them in a life of household chores.

The people of the Bible knew what it meant to be genuinely thankful when they had a clean supply of water, because it was the difference between life and death. For millions in the developing world the situation is no better now. The transience of a well dressing can remind you that the progress which means that our children do not die from drinking filth brings responsibilities with it.

How much? There is often a collecting box near the display to help fund the event, or for charities that provide clean water in the developing world.

The blessing lasts about 30 minutes, but there is usually a rural festival that fills the day and continues for a week. Planning lasts for several months, coming to a climax with a large group working against the clock with living plants.

Don't!

Don't leave it until the end of the week. See the well dressing at its best on the first day.

Who says?

Why did Jesus refer to the grace of the Holy Spirit under the name of water? Because through water all plants and animals live. The rain comes down from heaven, and though it comes in one form, its effects have various results . . . It turns white in the lily, red in the rose, and purple in the violet.
Cyril, bishop of Jerusalem, 315–386

You are most likely to think

In a tap, in a bottle, in a glass, in a shower, in a hose, in a cistern, in a kettle, in a radiator, in a rainfall – thank you, thank you, thank you!

You are least likely to think

I'd like to see the Damien Hurst version.

To help you reflect

The streams of God are filled with water
to provide the people with grain,
for so you have ordained it.
You drench its furrows and level its ridges;
you soften it with showers and bless its crops.
You crown the year with your bounty.
Psalm 65.8–11

[Hagar put Ishmael] under one of the bushes. Then she went off and sat down nearby, about a bowshot away, for she thought, 'I cannot watch the boy die' . . . She began to sob. God heard the boy crying, and the angel of God called to Hagar from heaven and said to her, 'What is the matter, Hagar? Do not be afraid . . . ' Then God opened her eyes and she saw a well of water. So she went and filled the skin with water and gave the boy a drink.
Genesis 21.15–20

The date I attended a well dressing

Where?

What was the design and wording?

What I will remember between here and heaven

177

89 Imagine yourself into a Bible story

HOW? Choose a single event from one of the narrative sections of the Bible. You are going to imagine yourself to be a witness to it, so select one in which many people were observing – possibly a resurrection appearance of Jesus, the occasion of a miracle, or an episode from the trek of the Hebrews through the wilderness. Read and familiarize yourself with the story.

Then shut your eyes and, in your imagination, see what is happening as if you were one of the people involved in it. Enter the story as an active participant, but one with an incidental part to play. Feel the sand beneath your sandals, smell the sea, hear the conversation, sense the sun on your head, taste the food. Let the story unfold in your mind at the same pace that it did when it originally happened. Work out the emotions that are being experienced by the people involved. If characters speak to you, give an appropriate answer. If they come toward you, move in response.

Be particularly aware of how you react to Jesus, or to the main characters. After several minutes, imagine yourself leaving the scene and walking away, then walk yourself back into the reality of the 21st century. Ask yourself what you noticed that you had not been aware of before.

This visualization of Bible stories was a style of meditation advocated by Ignatius of Loyola, the founder of the Society of Jesus (Jesuits), who lived in the 16th century.

HOW EXTREME?

Here → **❶** ② ③ ④ ⑤ → Heaven

What should I expect?

To start with, you will find yourself an observer, seeing the stories at a distance, like a film. However, as you get used to contemplating stories in this way, it becomes more natural to place yourself in the thick of events, becoming part of the action.

There is no need to try to analyse the event intellectually, or gather insights to share with others. Instead, apprehend it through your sense of smell, taste, and other feelings, so that you are more intrigued by its reality than its meaning. Ask questions of the characters, and find out what they say to you as the written word of the Bible becomes a living presence. They won't give you specific advice about what to do in your present-day circumstances, and you may be completely wrong about what you imagine, but you should find yourself more excited by the authenticity of events of many centuries ago than if you simply hear the stories read.

Think afterwards about what difference it would make if the presence of Jesus, saying and doing the things you have just imagined, was a reality.

You are most likely to think

Some lucky people really did get close enough to Jesus to brush against his cloak and hear his stomach rumble.

 You are least likely to think

Those Bible dudes had it cushy!

Don't!

Don't change the ending of the story, even if you can think of a better conclusion, or allow those in your retelling of the story to do something out of character.

 Who says?

The heart is commonly reached, not through reason, but through the imagination. By means of direct impressions, by the testimony of facts and events, by history, by description. Persons influence us, voices melt us, looks subdue us, deeds inflame us.
John Henry Newman, cardinal, 1801–1890

To help you reflect

The word of God is living and active. Sharper than any double edged sword, it penetrates even to dividing soul and spirit, joints and marrow; it judges the thoughts and attitudes of the heart.
Hebrews 4.12

Jesus told [Thomas], 'Because you have seen me, you have believed; blessed are those who have not seen and yet have believed.'
John 20.29

The date I imagined myself into a Bible story

The story I meditated on

Things I noticed about the story for the first time

What I will remember between here and heaven

90 Discover Celtic Christianity

HOW? Church leaders met at Whitby in 664 to seek God's will about the future of Christianity in Britain. They chose to follow the way the faith was practised in mainland Europe. But before Augustine arrived from Rome to convert England, Jesus had been worshipped on these islands for many years following the practices of missionaries who had come from Ireland via Scotland and north-east England.

In recent decades this Celtic form of Christianity has been rediscovered, because many issues that were important to the believers of the time have emerged again – for instance, the need to protect the earth, and the place of women in God's plan. There are many websites devoted to Celtic Christianity, and http://celtdigital.org/Christianity.html links to interesting articles. Introductory books include *Exploring Celtic Spirituality* by Ray Simpson, *A Celtic Primer* by Brendan O'Malley, and devotional books by David Adam. A visit to the off-shore islands that were centres of Celtic Christianity, Lindisfarne and Iona, enables you to understand the context in which these traditions first thrived.

HOW EXTREME?

Here → ① **❷** ③ ④ ⑤ → Heaven

What should I expect?

Celtic Christianity is shaped by a love of nature, and by appreciation of art and music, all of which are a gift of God. There is no distinction between sacred and secular. Every aspect of work and play is full of potential to be a way of learning from and serving God.

Celtic Christians saw their life as a pilgrimage, and had a vivid sense of the unseen presence of God and Christians who had gone before them. They recognized God in every aspect of creation and human creativity, so their prayers were both earthy and poetic. There was time for contemplation as well as time for energetically making Jesus known. They cared for the environment, and were passionate to improve the lot of the world's vulnerable, poor and sick people. It came naturally to them to respect women's leadership as well as men's. No wonder their way of life has inspired today's Christians to apply their wisdom to this generation.

Who says?

[For Celtic Christians] the natural landscape was both a concrete reality where people lived and a doorway into another, spiritual world. The sense of living in a 'between place' enabled Celtic Christians to make connections between . . . the seen and the unseen, this world and a permanently present 'other' world.
Philip Sheldrake, theologian

How much?

David Adam's books, published by Triangle, cost from £5.99. *A Celtic Primer* is published by Canterbury Press at £15.99, and *Exploring Celtic Spirituality* by Kevin Mayhew at £9.99. The price of accommodation on Lindisfarne ranges from £27 to £70 per night. The typical cost of a week spent on Iona is £224, plus travel.

 Three or four hours of reading may lead to a fascination that transforms time rather than using it.

Don't!

Don't get stranded on Lindisfarne, which becomes an island at high tide. Check crossing times by clicking the 'Transport' link at www.northumberland.gov.uk.

 You are most likely to think

My faith is worthless if it does not have an impact on every aspect of the way I live on this planet.

 You are least likely to think

The experience of Christians who lived hundreds of years ago can't teach anything to this technological age.

To help you reflect

I pray that out of his glorious riches [God] may strengthen you with power through his Spirit in your inner being, so that Christ may dwell in your hearts through faith. And I pray that you, being rooted and established in love, may have power, together with all the saints, to grasp how wide and long and high and deep is the love of Christ.
Ephesians 3.16–18

Let the word of Christ dwell in you richly as you teach and admonish one another with all wisdom, and as you sing psalms, hymns and spiritual songs with gratitude in your hearts to God. And whatever you do, whether in word or deed, do it all in the name of the Lord Jesus, giving thanks to God the Father through him.
Colossians 3.15–17

	The date I found out about Celtic Christianity
	The most interesting discovery
	Elements that I could incorporate into my own life
	What I will remember between here and heaven

91 Take part in a Passover meal

HOW? For thousands of years the Jewish people have celebrated the Passover (or *Seder*) to commemorate their release from slavery in Egypt. It is at once a family meal, a history lesson and an act of worship. It was this supper that Jesus ate with his followers the night before he died, and Christians remember it through communion. Christians sometimes recognize the debt their faith owes to Judaism by holding a Passover meal on Maundy Thursday, either as a family or on a larger scale in church.

Nick Fawcett's book *Celebrating the Seder* (Kevin Mayhew) explains how to share this celebration. There are also instructions, recipes and reflections from a Christian perspective at www.christianseder.com, which has links to the words that are said in the liturgical part of the event (the *haggadah*) that are adapted in the light of Christian theology.

Invite guests of all ages and set the table for dinner. Add a bowl of salt water, parsley sprigs, three *matzah* (brittle, flat bread), *charoset* (puréed nuts, fruit and wine), horseradish, a hard boiled egg, a shank of lamb, a candle, wine glasses, and one more seat than the number you are expecting. Each person needs a copy of the *haggadah*, because there are words that everyone says together during the story of how God rescued his people many centuries ago and still upholds them lovingly today. The elements on the table are used to bring the story to life, and in the middle of the prayers and readings, the meal is served.

HOW EXTREME?

Here → ① ② ❸ ④ ⑤ → Heaven

What should I expect?

At the climax of his final Passover meal, Jesus told his followers to remember him by eating bread and drinking wine. From that has developed the Christian communion service, although the way bread and wine are used has changed beyond recognition. Sharing a Passover meal not only brings to life the roots of the faith in Judaism, it can also give a new richness to your appreciation of the Christian act of worship.

Every element of the ritual means something. The salt water recalls the tears of the Hebrews in slavery, the lamb calls to mind the animal that was sacrificed on the eve of their departure from Egypt, the bread is unleavened to recall the haste at which they left, the egg is a symbol of new life, and so on. The empty chair is traditionally left for Elijah, the great prophet of justice and hope. Christians can bring their own symbolism to the traditions, for instance seeing the Trinity in the three *matzah*, one of which Jesus described as his own body when he broke it in the presence of his followers. The wine toasts life, freedom, reconciliation and an end to oppression – the very things for which Jesus went to the cross.

How much?

Celebrating the Seder costs £12.99. Budget for the event in the same way that you would an ample dinner party.

The Passover is a leisurely event, so allow an entire evening and much of the day to preparing the unique foods.

Who says?

Passover affirms the great truth that liberty is the inalienable right of every human being . . . It is God's protest against unrighteousness.
Morris Joseph, North American Jewish theologian

You are most likely to think

This is the meal that Jesus ate in sadness and fear so that I can eat it today in joy and thankfulness.

You are least likely to think

Worship only counts when it's boring.

Don't!

Don't skimp the meal. You are worshipping God as much by eating as by praying.

To help you reflect

[Jesus] said to [his followers], 'I have eagerly desired to eat this Passover with you before I suffer. For I tell you, I will not eat it again until it finds fulfilment in the kingdom of God.'
Luke 22.15, 16

Christ, our Passover lamb, has been sacrificed. Therefore let us keep the Festival, not with the old yeast, the yeast of malice and wickedness, but with bread without yeast, the bread of sincerity and truth.
1 Corinthians 5.7, 8

The date I took part in a Passover meal

With whom?

The things I ate and drank

What I will remember between here and heaven

92 Write a prayer

HOW? Clarify the kind of prayer you are writing. It might be a prayer that simply tells God that you worship and revere him because of his nature; one that thanks him for something; one that asks for forgiveness for wrong things you (or your entire society) have done; or one that asks him to act in response to a need. Jot a few words about the subject to act as notes.

First, decide how to address God. For instance, if it is a prayer for forgiveness you might call him 'Merciful Lord' or another title that focuses on his compassion; a thankful prayer could begin, 'Generous God'. Then write what you want to say to God in straightforward words. There is no need to attempt phrases that sound clever, lofty or biblical. However, to write a prayer rather than improvise it gives you the chance to use words that are not simply chatty. As a guideline, use the kinds of words you would use in a letter. However, split up the sentences into phrases of eight to ten words, starting each on a new line at natural breaks, such as commas or new ideas.

For some people a prayer asking God to act is not complete unless it is rounded with a phrase such as, 'Through Jesus Christ our Lord.' This is not a requirement, though, and it is sufficient to write, 'Amen,' (meaning 'let it be so') which allows others to voice their sharing of the prayer.

HOW EXTREME?

Here → **❶** ② ③ ④ ⑤ → Heaven

What should I expect?

There are two advantages to a prayer that you write, rather than say – you can keep it, and you can share it. Keeping it means that in days (or even years) to come you can look back and recall the concerns that were important to bring before God at a particular time. This helps you become continuously aware of how God is responding to your prayers, either by changing you or by changing the world.

Sharing your prayer can happen when it is read aloud in the context of a church service, or simply when you show a friend what you are praying. For a church service, if you are leading prayers of intercession, read through what you have written and ask yourself whether it is something with which everyone in the congregation will be able to agree. Your task is to give them words that encourage them to take the needs of the world to the heart of God, so try to be engaging and create positive phrases that inspire people. The same is true of other ways in which you can share your prayer – on websites, in church magazines, or by email to your friends.

Nothing.

 This will vary, but 20 minutes invested in writing a short prayer will allow you to focus thoroughly on what you are saying to God, and open you to awareness of his response.

Don't!

Don't imagine that God is impressed by the quality of the writing – only by the sincerity of the prayer.

 Who says?

In a sense the country is one vast, secret web of prayer and, if the Son of Man were to return tomorrow, huge sections of the country would be prepared and ready.
Tom Davies, journalist and broadcaster

You are most likely to think

The extra thought that went into this prayer has helped me speak clearly to God, but it has also helped me listen to God.

 You are least likely to think

Now God will do just what I tell him to do.

To help you reflect

I urge, then, first of all, that requests, prayers, intercession and thanksgiving be made for everyone – for kings and all those in authority – that we may live peaceful and quiet lives in all godliness and holiness. This is good, and pleases God our Saviour.
1 Timothy 2.1–3

I will pray with my spirit, but I will also pray with my mind.
1 Corinthians 14.15

The date I wrote a prayer

The subject

The context in which I shared or prayed it

What I will remember between here and heaven

93 Explore religions you know little about

HOW? The Religion Facts website (www.religionfacts.com) presents information about 30 world religions, including Buddhism, Sikhism and Hinduism, in an objective way. (It stretches the definition of religion to include sects.) The major religions are described over many pages, covering their history, worship and scriptures. However, there are also concise résumés, with charts comparing facts and statistics.

The New Lion Handbook: The World's Religions covers indigenous and New Age religions as well as the major faiths. It is up to date with recent developments and examines how fundamentalism and secularism are shaping religion. From a Christian publishing house, it nevertheless presents religions objectively and without distortion, and describes the richness of experiencing faith rather than bare facts.

The St Mungo Museum of Religious Life and Art in Glasgow houses exhibitions that compare beliefs. Through artefacts, photographs and recordings it shows the way faith impacts on the day-to-day life of adherents of the six largest religions. The museum is open daily from 10am to 5pm (www.glasgowmuseums.com).

HOW EXTREME?

Here → ① ② ❸ ④ ⑤ → Heaven

What should I expect?

Researching religions through books is engrossing, but merely knowing the facts does not give you a sense of the hope, healing and love that those who practise them find. Your discoveries will be greatly enhanced when you befriend someone whose life is shaped by worshipping and obeying God through adherence to their religion.

All religions are seeking answers to the same fundamental questions: How have we come to be here? What is the purpose of human life? What is our destination when our bodies wear out? Expect to encounter people who have set their hearts on doing good, and are looking for strength through their faith in God to fulfil their lives and improve the world, now and eternally. As you discover this, the trivia about those who practise other religions (such as their dress and unfamiliar rituals) will become less significant than admiration for their desire to live in a way that pleases God.

How much?

The World's Religions (Christopher Partridge, Lion Hudson), costs £25. The Museum of Religious Life and Art and the online resources are free.

Both the book and the website are exhaustive, and require several evenings to read.

Don't!

Don't imagine that you can understand a religion by knowing all the facts about it. Only those who have said 'yes' to a belief system know it fully.

Who says?

The uniqueness of Christianity is in Jesus Christ. He is the stumbling block of all ideologies and religious systems . . . [He] deserves to be the goal and standard for individuals and humankind . . . I consider traditional religions, Islam and the other religious systems to be preparatory and even essential ground in the search for the Ultimate. But only Christianity has the terrible responsibility of pointing the way to that ultimate Identity, Foundation and Source of security.
John Mbiti, Kenyan theologian

You are most likely to think

No matter how big any religion is, God is bigger.

You are least likely to think

All religions are the same – just with different names for God.

To help you reflect

Paul . . . said: 'People of Athens! I see that in every way you are very religious. For as I walked around and looked carefully at your objects of worship, I even found an altar with this inscription: To an unknown God. Now what you worship as something unknown I am going to proclaim to you. The God who made the world and everything in it is the Lord of heaven and earth . . . He has given proof of this to everyone by raising [Jesus] from the dead.'
Acts 17.22–24, 31

The Lord will scatter you among the peoples, and only a few of you will survive among the nations to which the Lord will drive you. There you will worship gods of wood and stone made by human hands, which cannot see or hear or eat or smell. But if from there you seek the Lord your God, you will find him if you look for him with all your heart and with all your soul.
Deuteronomy 4.27–29

The date I explored other religions

Something new I discovered

Something that has given me hope

What I will remember between here and heaven

94 Find out what you are worth

HOW? Visit the Global Rich List at www.globalrichlist.com. Enter your annual salary, either in pounds or euros. A graph will then reveal where you fit on a scale between the richest and poorest people of the world. Using information from the World Bank's development research group, the website will calculate the number of people in the world who are poorer than you, and tell you the percentage of the world's richest people to which you belong.

Click on the link at the foot of the page to take you to a web page specific to the UK, and discover some of the ironies of the way the resources of the world are distributed.

HOW EXTREME?

Here → **❶** ② ③ ④ ⑤ → Heaven

What should I expect?

It comes as a shock to almost everyone that their income, no matter how modest, is very substantial indeed compared with the vast majority of the world. Halving or even quartering your income, which would dramatically change your way of life, makes virtually no difference to your place on the scale between the world's richest and poorest people.

Further research reveals greater ironies. The world's 225 richest people have a combined wealth that is the equivalent of the world's poorest 2.5 billion people. In 1820 the richest 20 per cent of the world's population received three times as much as the poorest 20 per cent. By 1960 it had escalated to a scandalous 30 times. However, in 2002, the richest received 114 times as much as the poorest.

The challenge that comes with knowing your true worth is to use the information in a worthwhile way. Logic would suggest that realizing you are among the very richest people of the world should lead to a deep content and generosity. However, experience shows that the sentiment most likely to be generated by wealth is a desire for slightly more wealth.

The way of Jesus is to be content no matter the circumstances in which you find yourself. He challenged his followers to measure their commitment to the Kingdom of God by selling everything and giving the proceeds to the poor. Ask yourself what would have to go if you discovered tomorrow that you had £1,000 per year less. And then £5,000 per year less. Expect God to put in your mind actions you could take in order to make the gulf between your way of life and that of someone living in poverty slightly less extreme.

How much?

£ Nothing. However, the discovery you make may have a dramatic impact on the way you arrange your finances. The Global Rich List will calculate how much you earn in an hour and suggest that you donate that sum to developing the world's poorest communities.

 Ten seconds.

Don't!

Don't use this as an excuse for a spending spree.

 Who says?

The real measure of our wealth is how much we would be worth if we lost all our money.
John Henry Jowett, preacher, 1841–1923

 You are most likely to think

I had no idea that the little I have is so much in comparison with others.

You are least likely to think

I deserve to be in this place on the scale between the richest and the poorest.

To help you reflect

Our desire is not that others might be relieved while you are hard pressed, but that there might be equality. At the present time your plenty will supply what they need, so that in turn their plenty will supply what you need. Then there will be equality, as it is written: 'He who gathered much did not have too much, and he who gathered little did not have too little.'
2 Corinthians 8.13–15

I ask of you, O Lord . . . Give me neither poverty nor riches, but give me only my daily bread. Otherwise, I may have too much and disown you and say, 'Who is the Lord?' Or I may become poor and steal, and so dishonour the name of my God.
Proverbs 30.7–9

 The date I found out my financial worth

 Exactly how many of the world's people are poorer than me?

The changes I will make as a result of what I have discovered

 What I will remember between here and heaven

95 Watch an eclipse of the sun

HOW? A total solar eclipse can be seen when the moon, on its orbit around the earth, comes between you and the sun. A dark, curving shadow appears to eat into the sun, giving it a crescent shape, then covering it completely, like a black disc surrounded by a ring of light. Day turns briefly to night as the moon's shadow falls on you. The temperature drops and birds begin to sing because they think it is dusk.

Total eclipses of the sun are rare and only visible from certain places on the earth's surface on any occasion. On 1 August 2008 one will be visible from Canada, Siberia and China. On 22 July 2009 it will be possible to see an eclipse in India, Nepal and China. The next will be on 11 July 2010, visible in the south Pacific, Chile and Argentina, and on 13 November 2012, in northern Australia. To see a total eclipse in the UK you will need to live until 2090, although a partial eclipse (less rare, but less spectacular) will be visible on 4 January 2011.

HOW EXTREME?

Here → ① ② ③ ❹ ⑤ → Heaven

What should I expect?

Ancient literature describes eclipses, but without understanding their cause. They are described as fearful events, associated with vengeful gods demanding that people change their wicked behaviour. The Old Testament anticipates the 'great and dreadful day of the Lord', which will bring about the destruction of God's enemies and the deliverance of his followers, taking place during an eclipse.

For those who observe an eclipse during this century, the wonder is equally great, even though the reason is known and the date foreseen. Why? Perhaps because it reminds us of the complexity of the universe that God has placed us in, about which we know so much and yet so little, and which is so orderly and yet constantly unpredictable.

 To see a total eclipse during the next few decades will involve travel outside Europe, so be prepared for considerable expense.

 Two to five minutes of complete darkness, after many days of mounting excitement.

Don't!

Don't look directly at the sun. If you do, the lens of your eye will act like a magnifying glass and burn a hole in the retina. The safest method to view an eclipse is to make a pinhole in a sheet of paper and allow it to cast the sun's image on a screen. Despite rumours, watching through smoked glass or exposed camera film is extremely dangerous. Filters made from aluminized mylar are sold in optical devices made specially for viewing the sun. The only part of an eclipse that is safe to look at with the naked eye is the few spectacular seconds of total darkness.

 You are most likely to think

This is an awesome moment, and reminds me that it was God who first drew light out of darkness.

 You are least likely to think

The gods are angry with us.

To help you reflect

The day of the Lord is near in the valley of
  decision.
The sun and moon will be darkened,
and the stars no longer shine.
The Lord will roar from Zion
and thunder from Jerusalem;
the earth and the sky will tremble.
But the Lord will be a refuge for his people,
a stronghold for the people of Israel.
Joel 3.14–16

[The Lord] carried me away in the Spirit to a mountain great and high, and showed me the Holy City, Jerusalem, coming down out of heaven from God. It shone with the glory of God . . . The city does not need the sun or the moon to shine on it, for the glory of God gives it light, and the Lamb is its lamp. The nations will walk by its light.
Revelation 21.10, 11, 22–24

 Who says?

No. It made me feel really, really small.
Neil Armstrong, the first human to walk on the surface of the moon. Noticing that he could blot out the Earth with his thumb, he was asked, 'Did that make you feel really big?'

The date, time and place I saw an eclipse of the sun

A sequence of drawings of what I saw

My emotions

What I will remember between here and heaven

191

96 Dance in the rain

HOW? No amount of planning will prepare you for this moment. One unusually warm summer evening, at the end of a long dry period, the rain will tumble and this will prove irresistible. It is unlikely that you will be alone (although no one should rule it out); it is more likely that you will be with friends who share faith and trust. As the climax of a conversation or activity that makes you feel glad to be alive, open the door of the house or leap out of the car and start jumping around. You don't need music or any kind of technique – just excitement. A shower, a hot drink and a change of clothes will protect you against any subsequent feeling of regret!

HOW EXTREME?

Here → ① ② ③ ❹ ⑤ → Heaven

What should I expect?

The legacy of the Puritans is that most people picture the Christian faith as requiring restraint and sacrifice. This, however, is only part of the story. There is an element of Christian experience that can only be expressed through spontaneity and exuberance. Spontaneity was a feature of Jesus' life (for which Zacchaeus will be eternally grateful) and so was exuberance (defending himself for feasting with Matthew when others thought he should be fasting). Jesus knew the moment for solitude and the moment for gaiety. In his letters to the churches in the years after Jesus' resurrection, Paul urges them on nine occasions to overflow – with joy, thankfulness, love and hope.

The recklessness of dancing in the rain for the sheer joy of being alive is a reflection of the recklessness of God in creating a world teeming with colour and variety, and then entrusting it to mere human beings. It will remind you why, on the verge of his death, Jesus prayed for his followers to have joy, not to have dignity. No matter what age you are, after doing this you will be younger!

 Who says?

There was taken away from men all fear of those who had formerly oppressed them. They celebrated brilliant festivals. All things were filled with light, and men formerly downcast looked at each other with smiling faces and beaming eyes. With dancing and hymns in city and country alike they gave honour first of all to God the King of the universe.
Eusebius of Caesarea, historian of the early years of the Christian Church, writing about the victory of Emperor Constantine, 260–330

How much?

 Nothing.

 Five minutes should see you elated and wet through!

Don't!

Don't overdo it and wake up with a cold. And don't get this book wet!

You are most likely to think

I'm singing in the rain, just singing in the rain. What a glorious feeling; I'm happy again!

You are least likely to think

Slow, slow, quick, quick, slow!

To help you reflect

The Lord will ransom [his people]. They will come and shout for joy on the heights of Zion; they will rejoice in the bounty of the Lord . . . They will be like a well-watered garden, and they will sorrow no more. Then maidens will dance and be glad, young men and old as well. I will turn their mourning into gladness; I will give them comfort and joy instead of sorrow.
Jeremiah 31.11–13

David, wearing a linen ephod, danced before the Lord with all his might, while he and the entire house of Israel brought up the ark of the Lord with shouts and the sound of trumpets. [His wife] Michal daughter of Saul watched from a window. And when she saw King David leaping and dancing before the Lord, she despised him in her heart . . . [She] came out to meet him and said, 'How the king of Israel has distinguished himself today, disrobing in the sight of the slave girls of his servants as any vulgar fellow would!' David said to Michal, 'It was before the Lord . . . I will celebrate before the Lord. I will become even more undignified than this, [but] I will be held in honour.'
2 Samuel 6.14, 15, 20–22

The date I danced in the rain

Where?

What made me so joyful that I did it?

What I will remember between here and heaven

97 Make your own Christmas cards

H O W ? Organize yourself at the end of November, deciding on a design and buying the materials you need. The simplest way to personalize Christmas cards is to choose a photograph of your family or a winter scene, have copies made (either prints or on a home computer) and paste them to the front of folded card. Create your own message, which can say something more relevant to the meaning of Christmas than most commercially produced cards, and print it using a word processing package or write it if you have fine handwriting.

There are many other ways of creating designs by building layers of coloured paper, shapes and pictures on folded card. Simple shapes that immediately suggest a Christian Christmas include crowns, angels, mangers and stars. Stickers and templates can be purchased to give a more professional appearance, but scissors and paste, glitter and tinsel produce a result that will be appreciated just as much.

More complex cards can be created with traditional craft techniques. Decoupage uses three identical pictures. The first is pasted on the card, and individual elements of the second and third pictures are cut out and attached to the first with adhesive pads to give a three-dimensional effect. Quilling makes thin strips of paper, curled and crimped, stand out from the card. Stencilling and embossing create the outline of a more intricate image.

The links at www.makingcards.co.uk offer many designs and suggestions, as well as advice and online shops. There is, however, no substitute for your imagination, which allows you to create a design that expresses what Christmas means to you.

HOW EXTREME?

Here → ① ② ❸ ④ ⑤ → Heaven

What should I expect?

The salvation of the world could not be bought; it could only be given. That is the meaning of Christmas. God invested everything of himself in the creation of Jesus, and in doing so took an incalculable risk in order to demonstrate the extent of his love. During the Christmas season, every time you make something instead of buying it, you share in a small way in the creativity of God that brought about the first Christmas.

In an age that values time more than money, making your own Christmas cards is a demonstration of the extent of care you have for your friends and family. It allows you to choose images and write words that express your own feelings about God taking human, vulnerable flesh, instead of settling for someone else's clichés. And the process slows you down sufficiently to think about and pray for each person for whom you make a card.

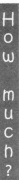

 A pack of 50 blank, pre-creased cards and envelopes costs £9. Stickers, glitter, ribbon and endless varieties of textured or shiny paper add between 10 and 20p to the cost of each card. 50 reprints of a single photo can be made for £7. Your own creativity is both free and priceless.

Allow six to eight hours to make sign and send 50 identical cards. The process becomes quicker as you progress. Teamwork halves the time and doubles the enjoyment.

 Who says?

I will honour Christmas in my heart, and try to keep it all year.
Charles Dickens, novelist, 1812–1870

 You are most likely to think

This year I gave people time and care, instead of money.

 You are least likely to think

My Christmas has just been a commercialized sham.

Don't!

Don't be overanxious about professionalism, because the charm of a home-made Christmas card lies in its wobbly edges.

To help you reflect

Finish the arrangements for the generous gift you had promised. Then it will be ready as a generous gift, not as one grudgingly given . . . Each of you should give what he has decided in his heart to give, not reluctantly or under compulsion, for God loves a cheerful giver.
2 Corinthians 9.5–7

Give, and it will be given to you. A good measure, pressed down, shaken together and running over, will be poured into your lap. For with the measure you use, it will be measured to you.
Luke 6.38

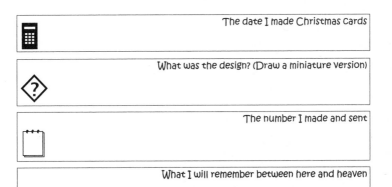

The date I made Christmas cards

What was the design? (Draw a miniature version)

The number I made and sent

What I will remember between here and heaven

98 Hug someone

HOW? The most common hugs take place between two people in an upright position. Beginners will require the following technical information:

The 'greeting hug' is the most familiar. In female/male or female/female combinations both huggers extend their arms at right angles to their bodies. They step forward and place their arms around each other's torso. By convention, the taller hugger positions his or her arms above those of the shorter. With practice, information about the expected duration can be given wordlessly through a glance before or a squeeze during the hug. Male/male instances differ in their brevity and by the accompaniment of back slapping (clarifying for observers the heterosexuality of the participants). In a church, a greeting hug takes place with the huggers one pace apart, creating an arch, to remove any possibility of the accidental convergence of genitals.

The 'comfort hug' is used to bring solace to someone close to you in a time of need. It follows the format described above, but with increased intensity and duration, and ministers at a depth that words cannot match. It is especially effective between parents and children.

The 'shoulder hug', usually reserved for lovers, has the arms encircling the neck instead of the back, thus locating the huggers' hearts in close proximity. Prior permission is vital for this intimate hug, which might otherwise be mistaken for attempted strangulation.

The 'seated hug' should only be attempted by agile people, since it involves the spine twisting in an unnatural way. More comfortable is the 'reverse hug'. The hugger approaches from behind and passes his or her hands around the huggee's waist. The element of surprise adds to the delight of this most affectionate of hugs, best reserved for those who share a long-established affection.

Multi-person variations include the 'sandwich hug', for three people of differing heights (often two parents and a child), in which the central person has the experience of being enveloped in fondness. The 'group hug' is formed by a circle of people with their arms around each other's waists. When performed by a sports team or at a party it expresses celebration and mutual joy.

HOW EXTREME?

Here → **❶** ② ③ ④ ⑤ → Heaven

What should I expect?

A good hug, generously offered and willingly received, is one of the most underrated experiences of life. It doesn't harm the environment, contains no calories, and leaves you feeling better both physically and spiritually. Treat it as paradigm of God's unmerited grace. (Oh, stuff that! Just enjoy it!)

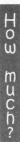
 Nothing.

 Longer. Please!

 You are most likely to think

This is the most fun you can ever have with your clothes on.

 You are least likely to think

Would this still be the most fun you can ever have without your clothes on?

Don't!

Don't indulge in the 'unwanted hug', in which a hugger persists despite the reluctance of the other person. This is abusive and recognizable by the unwilling party twisting her hip and tipping her head backward. And don't cause jealousy by leaving certain people unhugged.

Who says?

I will not play tug o'war,
I'd rather play hug o'war,
Where everyone hugs
instead of tugs,
Where everyone giggles
and rolls on the rug,
Where everyone kisses,
and everyone grins,
And everyone cuddles,
and everyone wins.
Shel Silverstein, children's poet, 1930–1999

To help you reflect

Greet one another with a kiss of love. Peace to all of you who are in Christ.
1 Peter 5.14

There is . . . a time to weep and a time to laugh,
a time to mourn and a time to dance,
a time to scatter stones and a time to gather them,
a time to embrace and a time to refrain.
Ecclesiastes 3.4, 5

The date I gave a memorable hug

Who?

What was the occasion?

What I will remember between here and heaven

99 Plan your funeral

HOW? Write a letter expressing things that are important to you about the way your life should be celebrated. In it, answer these questions: Where would you like the funeral to take place? Would you prefer to be buried or cremated? Do you want your organs made available for transplant? Is there anyone whom you would like to take part in the service? What mood should it have? What music would you appreciate being played? What Bible passages or poems could be read? Is there a symbol or action that would make the occasion unique? Would you like flowers, or would you prefer donations to be made to a charity – if so, which one? Do you have any requests about a lasting memorial?

Place these instructions with your will. Decide who you would like to take responsibility for the arrangements, and tell that person where they will be able to find the letter when the time comes. Think about who you would like to come to your funeral, and create a list of names and contact details so that the person arranging it does not miss anyone who should be informed.

An extensive guide to planning all the details, secular and religious, can be found at www.ifishoulddie.co.uk.

HOW EXTREME?

Here → ① ② ❸ ④ ⑤ → Heaven

What should I expect?

This is partly a gift to yourself, and partly a gift to the people you love. For you, it is an opportunity to work out what has been most significant in your personality or achievements, and to think of ways in which that can be expressed through music, words or actions. It is also a chance to witness to what God has meant to you during your life, and the hope you have about spending eternity with him. For your family and friends, who will be experiencing sadness or shock in the days after your death, it provides reassurance that they are doing something which would give you pleasure. Expect this to be a life-affirming exercise, making you even more appreciative of the people, words and music that God has given to enrich your life so far.

How much?

Making the plans costs nothing. However, the average cost of a funeral is now £1,347, with variations depending on region and the choice between cremation (cheaper) and interment.

Allow three hours to begin thinking through the issues, but revisit them from time to time.

Don't!

Don't use your funeral as an opportunity to settle old scores or send hidden messages. Sort those things out while you are alive.

 You are most likely to think

This will help the people I love to remember me with pleasure as well as with grief.

 You are least likely to think

I don't care, because I'll be dead anyway.

 Who says?

It's good to have to think about death. Death's what's real in life. It's just that we find ways to be busy. If we lived every day with death, we would live a different life and it would not necessarily be a depressing one. It would probably be more joyful. You know, I often lose the ability to prioritize. I'm rushing to get lunch for the children, and put the toilet paper on the toilet paper thing, and read the scripts, and it takes a kid getting sick or something to remember that it's not so important that there's stuff all over the floor and maybe, just maybe, you should play with your kids. People say that if we think about death all the time we'd go mad, but maybe we'd go sane.
Susan Sarandon, actress

To help you reflect

Blessings crown the head of the righteous . . . The memory of the righteous will be a blessing, but the name of the wicked will rot.
Proverbs 10.6–7

When the perishable has been clothed with the imperishable, and the mortal with immortality, then the saying that is written will come true: 'Death has been swallowed up in victory.' Where, O death, is your victory? Where, O death, is your sting?
1 Corinthians 15.54–55

The date I planned my funeral

The place I have lodged the instructions

The part my friends will enjoy most

What I will remember between here and heaven